Teaching Art & Crafts
in Elementary School

ANNETTE WOOD was trained at Homerton College, Cambridge, and after several years of teaching spent a year abroad traveling in India and Africa. She has taught a wide range of children in both traditional and modern English schools.

Teaching Art & Crafts in Elementary School

Annette Wood

A SPECTRUM BOOK

PRENTICE-HALL, INC., Englewood Cliffs, New Jersey 07632

Library of Congress Cataloging in Publication Data

Wood, Annette.
    Teaching art & crafts in elementary school.

    (A Spectrum Book)
    British ed. published in 1978 under title: Teaching
art & craft in junior & infant schools.
    1. Art—Study and teaching (Elementary).
2. Creative activities and seat work.   I. Title.
N350.W63   1981   372.5'044   80-14920
ISBN 0-13-891416-8
ISBN 0-13-891408-7 (pbk.)

Editorial/production supervision
and interior design by Eric Newman
Page layout by Mary Greey
Manufacturing buyer: Barbara A. Frick

Originally published as *Teaching Art & Craft in Junior & Infant Schools*
by Ward Lock Educational, London, England. © 1978 by Annette Wood.

10 9 8 7 6 5 4 3 2 1

COVER:
Mosaic by Lucien Hewetson,
Middle Street First School, Brighton, England.
Photograph by David Lloyd.

PRENTICE-HALL INTERNATIONAL, INC., London
PRENTICE-HALL OF AUSTRALIA PTY., LIMITED, Sydney
PRENTICE-HALL OF CANADA, LTD., Toronto
PRENTICE-HALL OF INDIA PRIVATE LIMITED, New Delhi
PRENTICE-HALL OF JAPAN, INC., Tokyo
PRENTICE-HALL OF SOUTHEAST ASIA PTE. LTD., Singapore
WHITEHALL BOOKS LIMITED, Wellington, New Zealand

Contents

Acknowledgments, xi

Introduction, 1

1 PUPPETS, 4

MAKING THE PUPPET, **4**   PUPPET CHARACTERS, **6**   THREE CLOTH BODIES TO
START WITH, **6**   THREE PUPPET HEADS, **7**   THREE EASY PUPPETS, **9**
PUPPETS MADE FROM GLOVES, **11**   SIMPLE PAPER PUPPETS, **13**   PAPER-
PLATE PUPPETS, **14**   PEANUT PUPPETS, **16**   PUPPETS FROM BOXES, **18**
SOCK PUPPETS, **19**   TALKING SNAKE WITH GUSSET MOUTH, **21**   HORSE
WITH GUSSET MOUTH, **22**   SHADOW-PUPPETS AND THEATER, **23**   MOVING
SHADOW-PUPPETS, **25**   SPOON AND SPATULA PUPPETS, **26**   POP-UP PUPPET, **28**
STRING-PUPPET DRAGON AND SNAKE, **29**

2 MASKS, 32

MASKS FROM BAGS AND BOXES, 33 CONE AND CYLINDER MASK, 35
PAPER-PLATE AND SHALLOW-CONE MASKS, 38 FOLDED MASKS, 39
POLYSTYRENE STICK-MASKS, 41 PAPIER-MÂCHÉ MASKS, 42

3 CRAYONS, 45

BULL'S-EYE PATTERNS, 46 CRAYON SGRAFFITO, 46 CUT-CRAYON
PATTERNS, 46 RESIST PATTERNS AND PICTURES, 48 TRANSPARENT
PICTURES, 48 TRANSFERS, 49 CRAYON BATIK, 50 SIMPLE RUBBINGS, 51
RUBBINGS FROM YOUR OWN DESIGN, 52 RUBBINGS FROM A PLASTER
BLOCK, 53

4 PICTURE MAKING, 54

MOSAIC AND COLOR-TONE PICTURES, 54 DOODLE LINES, 55 GRAINING
AND STIPPLING, 56 PICTURES USING BLEACH, 57 NUMBER PICTURES, 58
GRADED-SIZE PICTURES AND SPREAD-OUT SHAPES, 59 PAPER RELIEF
PICTURES, 60 CHESSBOARD PATTERNS AND PAPER WEAVING, 61
DRAWINGS FROM LIFE, 63 JUNK MONSTER, 64 CONCERTINA
CUTOUTS, 65

5 COLLAGE, 68

SILHOUETTE PICTURES, 69 COLORED-TISSUE MONTAGE, 69 RECESSION
PICTURES, 70 WALLPAPER PICTURES, 71 NEWSPAPER, MAGAZINE, AND
PAPER MONTAGE, 72 PHOTO MONTAGE, 73 STRING PICTURES, 74 RELIEF
COLLAGE FROM JUNK, 75 FABRIC COLLAGE, 76 TWO CHRISTMAS
PICTURES, 77

6 JUNK MODELS, 79

ORGANIZING JUNK BOXES, 79 BOATS, 80 MODELS FROM LARGE BOXES, 82
TOTEM POLE AND TRUCK, 84 PAPIER-MÂCHÉ BALLOON SHAPES—PIG AND
HUMPTY DUMPTY, 85 EASTER-CHICKS PICTURE, 86 FLYING BALLOONS, 87

PAPIER-MÂCHÉ BOWLS, **88** THINGS TO WEAR: HEADDRESS AND BINOCULARS, **89** SOLDIER'S OUTFIT, **90** HATS, **92** MODEL PEOPLE, **94** CONE AND WIRE FIGURES, **96** CHINESE FISH-KITE, **97** SIMPLE ANIMALS, **98** LARGE-SCALE MONSTER, **99** HANGING BIRD AND CAT, **100** FISH MOBILE, **102** FISH TANK, **103** LARGE-SCALE WIRE-AND-PAPIER-MÂCHÉ ELEPHANT, **104** MODEL SCENE, **106** CHRISTMAS DECORATIONS: POLYHEDRON AND SPHERE, **108** CHRISTMAS CHARACTERS, **110** A WISE KING, **111**

7 GREETING CARDS, 113

SIMPLE STUCK-ON PATTERNS, **114** CARD WITH OPEN WINDOWS, **115** CARD WITH A CONCERTINA FOLD, **116** SHAPED CARD, **117** WINDOW-FRAME CARD, **118** PADDED CARD, **119** REVOLVING CARD, **120** VALENTINE CARD, **121** EASTER CARD, **122** CHRISTMAS CARD, **123**

8 PRINTING, 126

PRINTING WITH PARTS OF THE BODY, **127** PRINTING WITH JUNK AND VEGETABLES, **128** PRINTING WITH STRING, **129** SYMMETRICAL PICTURES, **130** PRINTING FROM GLASS, **131** ROLLER PRINTING, **132** MONOPRINTING, **133** BLOCK PRINTING, **133** PRINTING WITH A PLASTER BLOCK OR POLYSTYRENE, **135** CARDBOARD-SILHOUETTE AND STENCIL PRINTING, **136** CARBON-PAPER PRINTING, **137** MARBLED PAPER, **138**

9 FABRIC DESIGN, 140

TIE-AND-DYE TECHNIQUE—KNOTTING, **141** MARBLING AND PLEATING, **142** TWISTING AND CLUMP TYING, **143** SEWING, **144** BATIK, **144**

10 POTTERY, 146

ORGANIZATION, **146** EQUIPMENT, **147** BASIC TECHNIQUES AND MATERIALS, **147** SOLID SHAPES, **149** SIMPLE MODELS, **150** THUMB POTS, **152** MOLDED DISHES, **154** TEXTURED PATTERNS ON TILES, **155** RESIST

x

PATTERNS, **157**   JEWELRY, **158**   FIGURE MODELING AND MORE ADVANCED
MODELS, **159**   MODEL SCENES, **161**   SLAB POTS, **162**   COIL POTS, **164**
SLIP DECORATION, **166**   GLAZING BY DIPPING AND POURING, **168**
GLAZE EFFECTS WITH COLORED GLASS, **170**

Acknowledgments

I would like to thank the pupils of Middle Street First School, Brighton; Woodstock Primary School, Oxford; Christchurch Primary School, Hanham; and Bromley Heath Junior School, Bristol, who made most of the art and craft work photographed in this book. I am also indebted to the headteachers and staff of these schools for all their help. In particular I am grateful to Mr. P. H. Mahoney, Mr. E. D. England, and Mrs. P. Wilson of Christchurch Primary School for the enthusiasm they showed in understanding many of the projects described in this book.

I owe a great deal to my sister Rosemary Taylor; my husband, Michael Wood; and Carol Horner for the help they gave me with the preparation of the text, and to Carolyn Mears, Janet Hall, and Mrs. J. Johnson, who contributed individual items of work to be photographed for the book. I am very grateful to David Dickinson, who was kind enough to take the photographs.

Finally I must thank my daughter Jenny, without whose cooperation this book could not have been written!

Teaching Art & Crafts in Elementary School

Introduction

This book is written for art and craft teachers, particularly nonspecialists. It is also written for anyone else involved in enjoying and developing creative skills with children.

Almost all children love to make things, and the benefit derived from doing so will be as much in the making as in the end product. The ideas contained in this book are suitable for children in elementary schools, but many of the activities will appeal to both younger and older children than these and to adults too! I have tried to include a wide variety of ideas and techniques, some traditional and some new, all of which have been tried and tested and have proved successful. I hope that there will be something for everyone to enjoy.

Some activities will require careful planning beforehand, but many others involve the use of simple materials and can therefore be quickly organized. In the sections entitled "Organization," I have tried to give some useful tips for the teacher. I have not attempted to describe how the whole class should be organized as this will depend on the individual teacher and the facilities available.

Many nonspecialists feel that they are incapable of teaching art and crafts properly because they are not artistic themselves. They assume that the children will be deprived of creative inspiration and that results will be unsatisfactory owing to their own lack of skill in the subject. There is no need for any teacher to feel this. The teacher's job is to be enthusiastic and encouraging. He or she provides the stimulus from which creative activities can develop. If the teacher allows the children freedom and opportunity to experiment and develop skills, they will gain confidence from small successes and will naturally progress to more ambitious projects. With the support and encouragement of the teacher, children with a flair and talent for art and craft work will want to exploit their skills to the fullest. In this situation, even very young children can produce surprisingly good results.

Art and craft work should not be treated as a subject isolated from the rest of the curriculum. It should be linked as often as possible to other aspects of the children's work and school life in general. Topic work, for example, can easily be organized to incorporate art, English, and math.

When a new material is introduced, the children should be allowed one or two periods of free play. This will enable them to become accustomed to handling the materials and have the opportunity to experiment and try out their own ideas. They will then be ready to learn more formal skills.

An idea or technique should be intro- duced as a starting point for the children's creativity. The introduction, whether it is a demonstration, an explanation, or a discussion centered on a visual aid brought in by the teacher, should be kept to a minimum. The most exciting and rewarding part for the children will be the first-hand experience of doing the thing themselves.

The wise art teacher will never have a fixed idea of what the finished work will look like, because this is in the hands of the children; and the element of the unknown will be exciting for both the teacher and the child. Don't always provide the solution to a problem of construction or design, but sometimes allow the children to work it out for themselves. During the introduction to a new technique, ask the children for their ideas about decoration and which tools are most suitable for which jobs.

This approach to creative work has many advantages. It teaches the children that they are free to use their own judgment and that they do not have to stick to one rigid pattern or idea. It allows full scope for creative talents to emerge and it can be very interesting for the teacher and the class to see many different interpretations of one theme.

If they wish to, the children should be allowed to look through this book and select for themselves the ideas and techniques that appeal to them. The ideas I have given can be used as guidelines to be interpreted in whatever way the children wish to use them. For this reason, I have not always specified the exact dimensions of the paper, cardboard, boxes, or materials needed for a particular activity. Instead, I have tried to leave scope for the ambitions and desires of the individual artist.

Good materials are essential if the children are to develop their ideas successfully. But this does not necessarily mean that the materials should be expensive or even that they have to be bought at all. Wrapping paper, paper bags, and wallpaper can often be used instead of more conventional art paper. Construction paper is cheap and colorful and is good for most things. Shelf (or kitchen) paper is also cheap, but it is much thinner than construction paper. For work that requires a less absorbent surface, a good-quality paper such as cartridge paper should be used. When paints are required, poster and acrylic paints give much bolder and more exciting effects than watercolor paints, so use these whenever possible except where it is essential to use a water-based paint, such as with several of the wax-crayon techniques. For sticking things together, a powder and water paste will fasten paper and lightweight objects, but heavier items will require a good-quality glue. One of the most important resources that I have constantly referred to in this book is a collection of junk stored in boxes. Many things that are left over from jobs done at home and are regarded as waste are very useful for art and craft work.

Using junk for making pictures and models encourages resourcefulness, both in selecting a suitable piece of junk for a particular job and in thinking of what can be done with the junk available. It is also the cheapest, most readily available, and easily stored source of materials for many craft activities.

Above all, art and crafts should be enjoyed by both teacher and pupil regardless of the standard of work achieved. All children are gifted in some way, and for the nonacademic child, art and craft work may be the outlet for creative talent that can provide a means of communication with others and give him or her the confidence to persevere with all other school subjects.

But, talented or not, all children should regard art and craft work as a pleasurable activity and a means of expression that gives satisfaction in the making and in the end product, however modest.

Puppets

Puppets can be used to illustrate nursery and number rhymes, poems, songs, and stories of all kinds. They have a great therapeutic value, creating opportunities for conversation with other puppets or people. A puppet can be a means of communication, an entertainment, and often a real comfort to a child.

Sophisticated materials are not necessary for puppet making, as puppets made from junk and scraps are often much more "alive" and fun to make.

The following are some suggestions for suitable junk items to use for the different features and limbs of puppets. Suggest some of these to the children, but always allow them to use their own ideas as well. Some suitable puppet characters are also given for easy reference.

MAKING THE PUPPET

Heads

Balls of all types and sizes; polystyrene blocks and spheres; blown-out eggshells; paper rolled into a ball and covered with a bag or a nylon stocking; Plasticine; papier-mâché over a small balloon; fruit and vegetables such as potatoes, turnips, oranges, and apples; circular cheese box;

cotton reels; liquid-dishwashing containers.

Eyes

Gummed paper; felt or material scraps; press studs; buttons; thumbtacks; sequins; acorn cups; bottle tops; dried peas.

Eyebrows

Pipe cleaners; string; wool; cotton; foam; felt.

Eyelashes

Curled paper; small feathers; sycamore wings; frayed string.

Noses

Gummed paper; cardboard and polystyrene pieces; corks; sections of egg cartons; twigs; dried beans; rose thorn; date pit; Ping-Pong ball.

Mouth

Pipe cleaner; material; felt; shoelace; soft candy.

Teeth

Paper straws; rice; polystyrene; foam rubber; cardboard; teeth from a comb.

Ears

Egg-carton segments; leaves; cardboard; felt.

Hair

Fur; cotton; straw; wool; raffia; frayed string; scouring pad; crepe paper; wood shavings; brush bristles; coconut fiber; corn on cob tassle.

Arms

Rolled paper with wire through the center to maintain shape; stuffed cloth tube; stocking or sock; pipe cleaner; lollipop stick; foam-rubber strips; knotted string.

Hands

Material; leather; ice-cream spoon; pipe cleaner twisted to make the shape; foam rubber cut to shape; straws; cane; pine needles pushed into a ball of Plasticine.

Legs

Concertina-folded paper strips; lollipop sticks; spatulas; pipe cleaners.

Feet

Split corks; leather scraps; small blocks of wood; carpet scraps.

PUPPET CHARACTERS

People

Queen; king; princess; prince; policeman; fireman; sailor; astronaut; nurse; football player; clown; ballet dancer; bride; choirboy; cowboy; Indian; Eskimo; Gypsy; Santa Claus; witch; magician; ghost; mermaid; angel; fairy; pirate; scarecrow; story and rhyme characters such as Red Riding Hood, Goldilocks, Cinderella, Robin Hood, and Humpty Dumpty.

Animals

Cat; dog; hamster; rabbit; horse; cow; sheep; pig; goat; donkey; lion; tiger; elephant; zebra; giraffe; reindeer; penguin; bear; panda; seal; camel; crocodile; octopus; kangaroo; squirrel; hedgehog; frog; caterpillar; butterfly; bee; snake; bat; ladybird; dragon; prehistoric monsters; unicorn; space creatures; owl; peacock.

THREE CLOTH BODIES TO START WITH

Organization

All material scraps should be stored in a cardboard box somewhere in the junkbox area. Rummage sales are a good source of attractive materials at very low cost. Alternatively use old handkerchiefs or an old sheet cut up into pieces of suitable size to make bodies for puppets.

Materials

Material; scissors; needle and thread or glue and brush.

Technique

The puppet bodies shown in Figures 1-1 and 1-2 are simply a square and a circle cut from cloth. The dotted lines show where slits and holes are made with scissors so that the fingers and thumb can protrude for the puppet's head and arms. All the raw edges of the cloth bodies can be folded under and a hem stitched or glued for a more professional finish.

The puppet body shown in Figure 1-3 is cut from a folded piece of cloth and sewn at the seams where indicated by the arrows. The cloth body is then turned inside out and a small opening is cut for the neck. The raw edges can be turned under and stitched or glued as before to make a hem if desired.

Heads for these bodies can be made using a variety of techniques, some of which have already been mentioned in

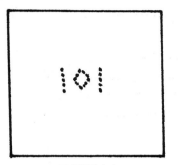

FIGURE 1-1

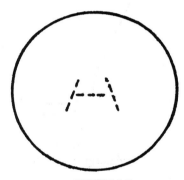

FIGURE 1-2

FIGURE 1-3

the section called "Making the Puppet." There are further suggestions for making puppet heads on the following pages.

THREE PUPPET HEADS

Organization

A spontaneous idea for a puppet may require a quickly made head. The bottle head is quickly made from a plastic bottle; other instant head shapes are balls, a blown eggshell, molded Plasticine, and carved soap. The newspaper head and the papier-mâché head require rather more planning and preparation.

Materials

Bottle head   Plastic bottle; scissors; glue and brush; junk-box scraps; white paper; junk.

Newspaper head   Newspaper; paste and brush; tape; scissors; wool scraps or cotton.

Papier-mâché head   Cardboard tube; box of tissues; bowl or pot of paste; scissors; glue and brush; junk-box scraps.

Technique

Bottle head   Using scissors or a sharp knife, cut off the neck and shoulders of an inverted plastic bottle about four inches (ten centimeters) from the end. Cut off the base of the bottle and glue it on top of the cut-off section as shown in Figure 1-4. The head shape can be covered with strips of white paper glued onto the plastic bottle to make a surface suitable for decoration with paints. Attach hair (see "Making the Puppet" for suggestions) to the head with glue. Features can be added by using a variety of materials from the junk boxes. The puppet head is supported by the index finger pushed through the neck of the bottle.

Newspaper head   Roll several sheets of newspaper into a tight roll, leaving a hole at one end for a finger to go in. Flatten the rest of the roll, and starting at the opposite end from the hole, bend the roll into sections, folding them over on top of each other until the shape shown in Figure 1-5 is achieved. Leave a short section of unfolded newspaper at the end with the hole so that a finger can be pushed through to support the head when the puppet is used. Secure the newspaper head shape with tape or strips of glued paper wrapped around it. Cover the head with a thick layer of paint, and

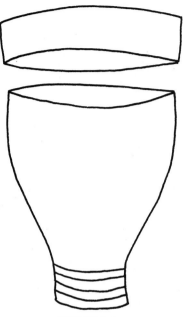

FIGURE 1-4
Making the bottle head

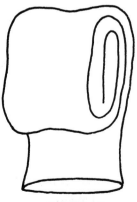

FIGURE 1-5
Making the newspaper head

when dry, paint on the facial features. Glue on strips of wool, curled paper, cotton or any of the other suggestions given for hair.

Papier-mâché head A detailed head and face with molded features can be made using a papier-mâché technique. Cut a section from a cardboard tube such as a toilet-paper roll or a narrower tube if this is availabe. Dip a tissue in a bowl of wallpaper paste or any powder paste and wrap it around the top of the cardboard tube. Build up the head and add papier-mâché features to the puppet by molding layer upon layer of pasted tissue into shape around the cardboard tube, leaving a section at the base of the tube for the neck. When the head is complete, allow the papier-mâché to dry thoroughly. The dry tissue will resemble the texture of skin. Decorate the head and face with paints and junk-box scraps.

THREE EASY PUPPETS

Organization

These three easily made puppets are a good introduction to puppet making. They demonstrate how effectively items from the junk boxes can be used to make interesting puppets.

Materials

Man Cardboard tube such as a toilet-paper roll; egg carton; cardboard; wool scraps; gummed paper; material; glue and brush; scissors.

Animal Paper bag; newspaper; string; gummed paper; cardboard; glue and brush; scissors.

Space creature Yogurt carton; material; cardboard; colored paper scraps; two buttons; glue and brush; scissors.

Technique

Man Cut a cardboard tube to the length required for the head. Cut out a circle of cardboard larger than the end of the tube and glue this onto one end of it. Cut out one section from an egg carton and glue this on top of the circle to make the hat. Glue scraps of wool onto the tube just below the hat, to resemble hair. Use gummed paper to make the facial features. Cut out a circle of material about one foot long (thirty centimeters) across and cut a hole at the center with the same circumference as the cardboard tube. Apply a layer of glue to the material all around the hole and attach the material to the inside rim of the tube at the lower end.

FIGURE 1-6
Man

FIGURE 1-7
Animal

Animal Roll some newspaper into a tight ball and push it into the end of a paper bag. Grip the outside of the bag underneath the newspaper ball and tie securely with string to hold the newspaper in place. Cut out ears from cardboard, allowing a small flap at the base with which to attach the ears to the head as shown in Figure 1-7. Glue the flaps of the cardboard ears and attach them on each side of the head. Facial features can be made from gummed paper or painted onto the puppet's face.

Space creature To make the space-creature puppet, cut out a circle of ma-terial and cut a hole in the middle the same size as the open end of an empty yogurt carton. Apply glue around the circumference of the hole on the material and attach it to the inner rim of the yogurt carton's open end. Cut out inter-esting ears from cardboard using the same technique as when making the animal puppet, and glue the ears onto the pot by their flaps. If the yogurt carton is patterned, use strips of plain white paper glued around it to cover the whole carton.

Make features from colored-paper scraps and glue these in position. Cut two strips of stiff cardboard and glue

FIGURE 1-8
Space creature

buttons or bottle tops onto one end of each strip to make antennae. When the glue is dry, attach the cardboard and button antennae to the top of the yogurt carton, using strong glue.

PUPPETS MADE FROM GLOVES

Organization

Gloves for making puppets can often be bought from rummage sales at little cost. When the children lose a glove or mitten, as so often happens, the remaining glove

or mitten can be donated to the junk box. The school lost-and-found box can also be a source of unwanted gloves after a suitable length of time is allowed for the gloves to be claimed.

Materials

Scraps of material, black felt, leather and fur; red glove; cotton; bottle top; glue and brush.

Technique

A puppet family and a finger mouse.
A glove can be used to make finger puppets. Features cut from material scraps are glued onto the fingers of the glove to create the characters in a family, ranging from grandmother down to the baby. Fur scraps or cotton can be used for hair. Hats and bonnets will add interest to the various characters in the family (Figure 1-9).

Individual puppets can also be made, such as the mouse shown in Figure 1-10. Its ears and tail are cut from scraps of leather and glued to its body in the positions shown. Its eyes are made from small scraps of material, sequins, or tiny buttons attached with glue. The mouse's whiskers are pipe cleaners pushed right through the end of the glove's fingertip.

FIGURE 1-9
Puppet family made from a glove

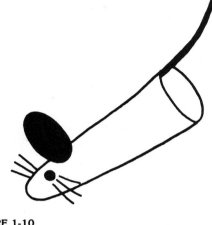

FIGURE 1-10
Finger mouse

Santa Claus Santa Claus is made from a red glove. The index and middle fingers are used for his legs. Cut out pieces of black felt for his belt and boots and use silver foil to make his buckle. Glue the felt and foil pieces onto the back of the glove in the correct positions. The facial features are made from scraps of material glued onto the glove. A cotton beard, moustache, hat trim, and boot tops complete the character. If arms are required,

FIGURE 1-11
Santa Claus

these can be made from material or felt scraps glued onto each side of the glove body.

A sack for Santa Claus can be made from a small piece of material and filled with small items from the junkbox to resemble a sack full of toys.

SIMPLE PAPER PUPPETS

Organization

Remind the children that when they have finished any craft activities, they must clean up their work area thoroughly. Tops must be put on paints and glue pots and brushes must be washed. Ensure that the children return leftover pieces of colored, gummed, and fancy papers to the appropriate junk box, as even tiny pieces can be used for decorating many types of puppets.

Materials

Loop puppet   Magazine; paper; scissors; glue and brush.

Envelope puppet   Envelope; gummed paper; scissors.

Paper-bag puppet   Paper bag; gummed paper; scissors; paint or crayons.

Technique

Loop puppet   Look through a magazine and choose a picture of a human or an animal. Cut out a strip of paper about one-third of an inch (one centimeter) wide and glue it onto the back of the cutout puppet to make a loop as shown in Figure 1-12. A finger is put through the loop to manipulate the puppet. To make a more sturdy puppet, mount the magazine cutout on thin cardbard and also make the loop from cardboard.

Envelope puppet   Seal an envelope and slit it open along one of the shorter sides. This provides an opening in which to put

FIGURE 1-12
Loop puppet

FIGURE 1-13
Envelope puppet

FIGURE 1-14
Paper-bag puppet

a hand when the puppet is used. Decorate the envelope with cutout gummed-paper shapes to make the features.

Paper-bag puppet This puppet is made from a paper bag with the opening at the bottom for a hand. Decorate the bag with gummed paper, cutout shapes, paints, or crayons to create a human or animal face. The addition of ears to the puppet will improve the rather rigid and formal shape of the paper bag.

PAPER-PLATE PUPPETS

Organization

Lollipop sticks can be used to support the paper-plate puppets, but wooden spatulas are broader and easier to handle. They can be bought as tongue depressors from large pharmacies in reasonably large and economical quantities and are well worth the investment as they can be used for many different things.

Materials

Sad or happy face Two paper plates; paints and brush; gummed paper; spatula; cotton or fur; glue and brush.

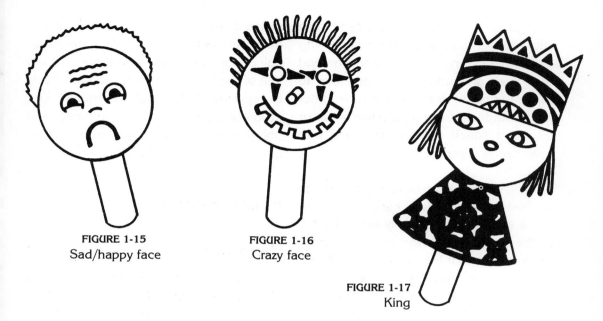

FIGURE 1-15
Sad/happy face

FIGURE 1-16
Crazy face

FIGURE 1-17
King

Crazy face Paper plate; thick wool; cork; polystyrene; polystyrene cutter; polystyrene cement; glue and brush; scissors.

King Paper plate; aluminum foil; cardboard; thick wool; doily; spatula; scissors; shiny candy or gum wrappers; gummed paper or paints and brush; glue and brush.

Technique

Sad or happy face Apply glue to one end of the spatula and attach it to the back of one of the paper plates. Glue the back of the second plate onto the back of the first plate to create a second face for decoration. Use paints, sticky paper, or junk-box scraps to create features on the plates. Make a happy face on one side and a sad face on the reverse side. Glue cotton or fur hair on the top half of the plates in the space between the two rims. This puppet is useful for telling stories in which the fate of the character changes dramatically.

Crazy face Attach the spatula to the paper plate as described above. Cut out strips of very thick wool and glue these into position for hair. Cut out eyes from sticky paper and stick these on, using glue if necessary. Apply glue to one end of a cork and attach it to the face to make the nose. Use a polystyrene cutter to cut out teeth from a polystyrene tile or dish and attach them to the face with polystyrene cement.

King Attach a spatula to a plate as described for the sad or happy face. Cut out a section from a doily and attach it to the back of the lower rim of the plate as shown so that the join does not show. Glue strips of very thick wool onto the sides of the plate near the top to resemble hair. Add facial features by using gummed paper or paints. Cut out a crown from thin cardboard and apply glue all over one side of it. Lay a piece of aluminum foil large enough to cover this crown on top of it, and press the foil down lightly. Where the foil overlaps the cardboard, cut slits from the outside of the foil to the edge of the cardboard. Fold over the cut foil pieces and glue them to the back of the crown. Cut out further decorations for the crown from the shiny candy or gum wrappers and glue these in position. Glue the crown onto the king's head to cover the area where the hair is joined to the face.

It is possible to give a paper-plate puppet an open mouth by using two plates. Fold one of the plates in half and glue the back of one half to the lower half of the other plate so that the unglued half of the folded plate hangs down freely to represent the top of the mouth. The inside of the mouth can be painted, and polystyrene or cardboard teeth can be glued on at the edges.

PEANUT PUPPETS

Organization

Often the children or their parents will be pleased to provide the teacher with a variety of interesting materials which are not always available from school supplies. For example, perhaps one member of the class knows someone who has a grocery who can provide a bag of peanuts for making these puppets.

Materials

Peanuts; cocktail sticks; leather; fur and material scraps; scissors; glue and brush; black felt-tip pen.

Technique

Push one end of a cocktail stick into a complete peanut shell to make a handle for the puppet. Decorate the peanut with

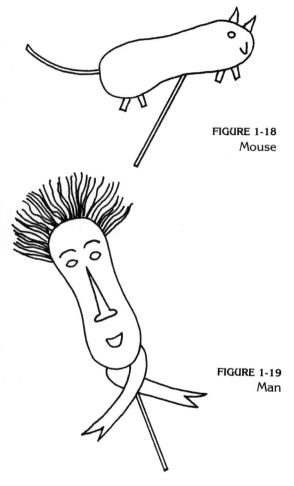

FIGURE 1-18
Mouse

FIGURE 1-19
Man

man puppet has a scarf cut from material, wrapped around the lower end of his peanut face, and glued into position. His eyes, nose, and mouth are cut from material scraps and glued onto his face. A small piece of fur is glued to the top of his head to make the hair, and this completes the character.

The flying bird is decorated with leather scraps cut into shapes to resemble its wings and tail. Its eyes and beak are cut from material and glued in position on its head. For an open beak, cut a diamond-shaped piece of material or card, fold it in half, and glue it at the fold onto the peanut.

FIGURE 1-20
Bird

scraps from the junk box glued on securely. The mouse puppet has ears, legs, and tail cut from scraps of leather. Small circles of material are glued onto the face for its eyes and a black felt-tip pen is used to draw its nose and mouth. The

PUPPETS FROM BOXES

Organization

Before the children begin any craft, encourage them to get all the necessary equipment together before they start and to prepare their work surfaces by covering them with newspaper or a plastic cloth.

Materials

Man   One box large enough to cover the hand, such as a small cereal box; several smaller boxes; string; round cheese box; cardboard; scissors; glue and brush.

Clown   Matchbox; Ping-Pong ball; material or felt scraps; four buttons; spatula; scissors; glue and brush.

Technique

Man   Cut away one section of the large box to allow the hand to go inside when the puppet is used. Cut a piece of string long enough to make the two arms of the puppet and to pass across the top of the box. Make holes on either sides of the box near to the top and thread the string through them, leaving a good

FIGURE 1-21
Man

length hanging on each side for the arms. Select two small boxes and thread these onto one of the string arms through holes made in opposite sides of the boxes. Dab some glue where the string passes through the holes to hold the boxes in position. Cut out a hand shape from cardboard and attach it to the end of the string with glue. Repeat this procedure for the other arm and make the two legs in the same way, cutting out feet from the cardboard to attach to each leg. Glue a round cheese box on top of the large box for the head and decorate the face with felt, material, and paper scraps glued securely in position. Some ears and hair cut from cardboard and attached to the head will add interest. When used, the puppet's limbs will swing about when the hand is moved and twisted inside the box.

Clown Attach a spatula to the back of a matchbox with strong glue and cover all the surfaces of the matchbox with material or felt cut to size and glued in place. Thick paint could also be used to decorate it. Cut out strips of felt for the puppet's arms and legs and glue these in position at the top and bottom of the matchbox. Glue a button at each end of the four limbs to represent hands and feet. Apply a thick blob of glue to the top of the matchbox at the center. Press a Ping-Pong ball into the glue. Lay the puppet on a flat surface so that the Ping-Pong ball is held in position during drying. When thoroughly dry, design a face for the Ping-Pong ball by gluing material and felt shapes onto it. Make a beard from a scrap of fur and a triangular hat from thick felt cut to shape or cardboard covered with thinner felt. Glue these into position on the Ping-Pong ball, and the puppet is complete. Swing him around with the spatula and see him dance!

FIGURE 1-22
Clown

SOCK PUPPETS

Organization

As with gloves, socks can be bought cheaply from rummage sales and washed before they are made into puppets. The whole sock can be worn on the arm to make a body for the puppet, which can be decorated. This gives the puppet plenty of flexibility and scope for movement.

Materials

Duck   White or yellow sock; cardboard; two buttons; stapler and two staples.

Dog   Colored sock; yogurt carton; black felt and leather scraps; scrap of red material or felt; scissors; glue and brush.

Technique

Duck   This puppet is quick and easy to make. Cut a beak shape from cardboard and staple it in position on the end of a white or yellow sock. Paint the beak yellow, orange, or any other suitable color. Sew or glue two buttons onto the sock to represent eyes.

Dog   Insert the yogurt carton into the open end of the sock and push it right down to the toe. Cut out the dog's features from material, leather, and felt scraps and glue these in position on the sock. A black leather nose and a red felt tongue will add interest to the puppet. To make stiff ears, cut out ear shapes from cardboard and cover the cardboard on

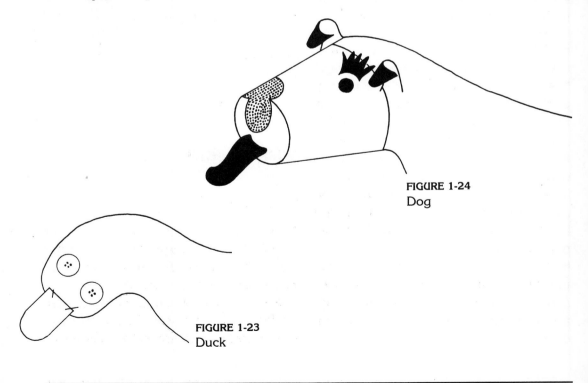

FIGURE 1-24
Dog

FIGURE 1-23
Duck

both sides with material cut to the same size. Glue the material to the cardboard and bend the ears over at the pointed ends to make them look floppy. Fold back a small section at the base of each ear and glue these on each side of the dog's head.

TALKING SNAKE WITH GUSSET MOUTH

Organization

It is helpful if the teacher can make a puppet of this kind before the lesson to use as a visual aid. As well as giving the children as idea of what can be achieved, this will help the teacher to foresee what difficulties the children may encounter when they make the puppets themselves.

Materials

Sock; scraps of material and felt; buttons; scrap of fur or thick wool strands, scissors; glue and brush; needle and thread.

Technique

The gusset is a piece of material which is inserted into the toe of the sock to make a mouth. The mouth can then open and close to make the puppet

"talk." Cut around the outside edge of the toe of the sock as shown in Figure 1-25 and fold the lower half back to meet the heel of the sock. Cut out a piece of material to make the gusset, which is fitted inside the opening as shown in Figure 1-25. (The shaded area in the illustration represents the gusset.) Neatly stitch the edge of the gusset to the open toe of the sock. This forms the mouth of the puppet. When the puppeteer's arm is pushed into the sock, the fingers control the upper section of the gusset mouth and the thumb controls the lower section.

Decorate the face and body of the puppet with material, cutout felt scraps, or other junk items glued into position. To make the puppet into a snake, a long

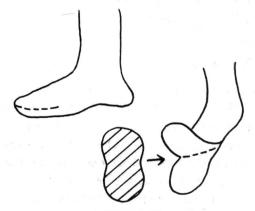

FIGURE 1-25

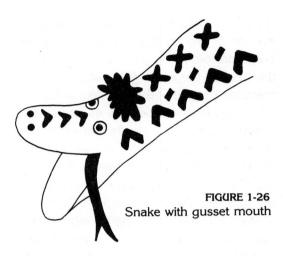

FIGURE 1-26
Snake with gusset mouth

brightly colored tongue is glued just inside its mouth. A scrap of fur or a bundle of thick wool strands tied together makes a topknot for the snake's head, and buttons can be added for his eyes.

HORSE WITH GUSSET MOUTH

Organization

Plays based on Aesop's Fables, the story of Noah's Ark, or children's own animal stories are enhanced by the use of animal puppets of this kind. These puppets are particularly mobile with their long, flexible bodies and their expressive mouths. The type of conventional materials that are sold in stores for stuffing toys and puppets can be expensive, so encourage the children to bring in old socks from home for this purpose.

Materials

Sock; pink material or felt; old stockings; yogurt carton; needle and thread; felt scraps; wool; foam rubber; scissors; glue and brush; bradawl or equivalent.

Technique

Make a pink gusset mouth in a sock as previously described. Stuff the toe of the sock with old stockings pushed into the upper and lower parts of the mouth made by the gusset. Make several holes around the upper rim of a yogurt carton with a bradawl or similar boring tool. Push the carton down into the sock as far as the stuffing. If the carton does not hold the stuffing in place, secure it by holding it in position against the stuffing, and using a needle and cotton of the same color as the sock, stitch through the sock and the holes previously made in the carton.

Decorate the horse's face with ears and eyes cut from felt and glued on. Use wool scraps and glue to attach a forelock and mane to the puppet. The teeth are cut from pink foam rubber and glued just inside the mouth.

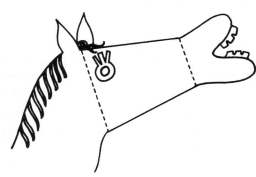

FIGURE 1-27
Dotted line shows the position of the
yogurt carton inside the sock

SHADOW-PUPPETS
AND THEATER

Organization

The children will enjoy using the shadow-puppets in the theater. At first, the children should use their puppets spontaneously, inventing dialogue as they go along. Later, they should be encouraged to write scripts for short plays to be practiced and then performed to an audience of other children in the class.

Materials

Shadow-puppet theater   Cardboard box; thin material; scissors; glue and brush; flashlight.

Girl and fish shadow-puppets   Cardboard; scissors; doily; red acetate; glue and brush; stick.

Technique

Shadow-puppet theater   Cut off the opening flaps of a large cardboard box; then cut away the base of it, leaving a border of about two inches (five centimeters) all around the edge so that it resembles a television screen. Use some fairly transparent material such as fine linen or an old cotton sheet to make a screen the same size as the base of the box. Glue this piece of material inside the base of the box, attaching the four sides of the material to the cardboard border.

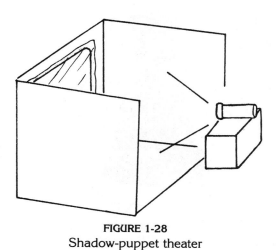

FIGURE 1-28
Shadow-puppet theater

Turn the box on its side and shine a flashlight through the screen from the back of the box. The flashlight can be placed on a pile of books while the puppet show is in progress. Sticks are used to hold the puppets against the back of the screen. As a temporary measure, the puppets can perform against the back of thin blinds when they are drawn down over the windows on a sunny day.

Girl and fish shadow-puppets Cut out the shape of a girl or fish from cardboard. Cut away some sections from the basic shape as shown in Figures 1-29 and 1-30, leaving a border around the edge of the shape.

Decorate the cut-away sections of the puppets by gluing a section of a doily onto the back of the girl and some transparent colored paper such as red acetate onto the back of the fish, in each case trimming off any excess protruding over the edge of the puppet.

Dip the end of a stick in glue and attach it at right angles to the back of the puppet on a suitable section of the cardboard. Hold it in position while the glue dries; then the puppet is ready to use.

FIGURE 1-29
Girl shadow-puppet

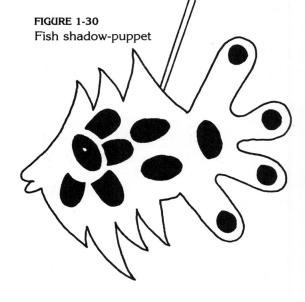

FIGURE 1-30
Fish shadow-puppet

MOVING SHADOW-PUPPETS

Organization

Bundles of suitably sized sticks can be purchased quite cheaply from gardening stores. They are a good investment as they have many uses in craft work. Make sure the children use sticks sensibly to avoid accidents.

Materials

Bird Cardboard; fur fabric; material scraps; feathers; silver foil; two sticks; scissors; glue and brush.

Dog Cardboard; scissors; two paper fasteners; stick; glue and brush.

Technique

Bird shadow-puppet Cut out a head, neck, and body for the bird from one piece of fur fabric. Glue cardboard circles onto the back of the fabric head and body to support the shape. Use material scraps to make a beak and eye and attach these to the head of the bird with glue. Two feathers can be glued onto the back of the body for a tail. Cut out the bird's legs from cardboard, cover them with silver foil, and attach the legs to the back of the body with glue. Turn the bird over so that the back is uppermost and attach two sticks to the puppet, one at the head and one on the body. The sticks may be held upright to support the puppet as shown in Figure 1-31, or if the puppet is to be used with the shadow-puppet theater, attach them to the puppet's head and body at right angles. A two-stick puppet of this kind is capable of plenty of movement while still being easy to control.

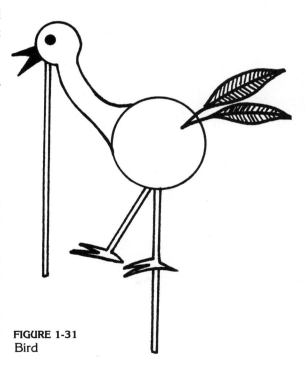

FIGURE 1-31
Bird

FIGURE 1-32
Dog

Dog shadow-puppet Cut out the body of the dog from cardboard, omitting the legs. Decorate the face and body with felt-tip pens or material scraps. Draw the pattern for the legs as shown in Figure 1-32 on two circles of cardboard and cut them out. Attach the legs to the body through the center of the circle with paper fasteners so that the legs revolve easily. Dip the end of a stick in glue and attach it at right angles to the back of the puppet. Hold the stick in position while the glue dries; then the puppet is complete. When the dog is moved along a flat surface, its legs will revolve so that it looks as if the dog is walking.

SPOON AND SPATULA PUPPETS

Organization

New wooden spoons are expensive, so look for old ones in junk shops and at rummage sales. If badly discolored, the spoon can be dipped in pink, glossy, leadfree paint and allowed to dry before it is made into the puppet. Both puppets are suitable for very young children to make.

Materials

Spoon puppet Wooden spoon; material; scissors; rubber band or string; strip of braid or ribbon; paints and brush or felt scraps; fur fabric or cotton; glue and brush.

Spatula puppet Spatula; felt; fur and material scraps; wool; cardboard; colored and gummed paper; wire; pink foam rubber; glue and brush.

Technique

Spoon puppet Wooden spoon; material; scissors; rubber band or string; strip of braid or ribbon; paint and brush or felt scraps; fur fabric or cotton; glue and brush.

Spatula puppet Spatula; felt; fur and material scraps; wool; cardboard; colored gummed paper; wire; pink foam rubber; glue and brush.

Technique

Spoon puppet Cut a circle from material and make a hole at the center, using scissors. The hole should be large enough for the handle of the spoon to pass through. Put the handle through the hole and fasten the material just below the bowl of the spoon with a rubber band or string. Tie a narrow strip of material, braid, or ribbon around the puppet's neck to hide the rubber band. Paint the features of the face with very thick paint, or cut out the features from felt and glue them in place. Cut out a strip of fur fabric and glue it around the top edge of the spoon to resemble hair. For a more professional finish, the hem of the puppet's dress can be turned under and glued, stitched, or trimmed with pinking shears.

Spatula puppet Cut out facial features from felt, fur, material, or junk-box scraps or simply use colored, gummed paper.

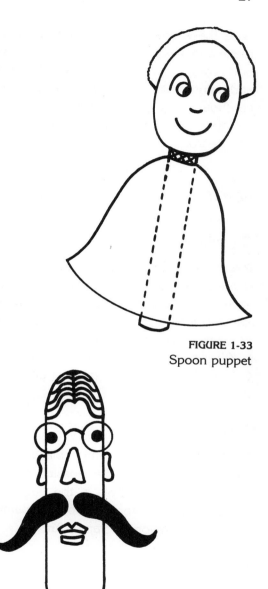

FIGURE 1-33
Spoon puppet

FIGURE 1-34
Spatula puppet

Glue these shapes onto the spatula to make a face. Glasses can be made from odd scraps of wire or cut from cardboard and painted black. Ears can be cut from cardboard or pink foam rubber. Wool or fur fabric makes a good moustache, hair, and beard.

POP-UP PUPPET

Organization

Ping-Pong balls that have been split or dented are no use for table tennis, so save them for craft work. Yogurt cartons are useful for containing small quanities of paint, paste, and glue as well as for making puppets and models. Collect a variety of sizes of plastic pots for different uses.

Materials

Stick; Ping-Pong ball; large plastic pot; glue and brush; scissors; possibly a bradawl for making a hole in the pot; material; ribbon or braid; cardboard; paints and brush; crayons; scrap of fur.

Technique

The head, arms, and cloth body of the pop-up puppet shown in Figure 1-35 must be small enough to fit inside a large

FIGURE 1-35

plastic pot or tub. To make the puppet, make a hole in a Ping-Pong ball with the pointed ends of a pair of scissors. Push a stick into the ball and dab glue all around where the stick is in contact with the ball. This holds the ball in position. Cut out a circle of material rather larger than the open end of the plastic pot. Make a hole at the center of the material and push the end of the stick through the hole until the Ping-Pong ball almost reaches the material. Fasten the material in place with a piece of braid or ribbon. Cut out two small arms and hands from cardboard. Decorate them with paints or crayons and staple or glue them on each side of the puppet's cloth body. Paint a surprised expression on the Ping-Pong ball face and glue a scrap of fur on the top for hair. Decorate the outside of the plastic pot with thick paint or a piece of material attached to the pot with glue.

Make a hole in the base of the pot for the stick to pass through, carefully using the pointed end of a pair of scissors or a bradawl. Push the stick through the hole in the pot and glue the lower, outer edge of the material circle to the inside rim of the plastic pot. When the stick is pulled down, the puppet disappears inside the pot. When the stick is pushed up quickly, the puppet leaps out of its hiding place.

STRING-PUPPET DRAGON AND SNAKE

Organization

To use these puppets, turn a table or desk on its side. The table or desk top can then be used as a backdrop for the puppets and can be suitably decorated to suit the theme of the play. Background pictures can be painted and held in position on the table top with cellophane tape. Quick scene changes are possible by simply folding back a picture to reveal another one underneath.

Materials

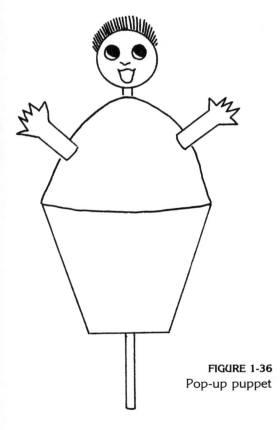

FIGURE 1-36
Pop-up puppet

Dragon Material; scissors; cardboard egg cartons; paints and brush; glue and brush; string.

Snake   Stocking; material scraps; old stockings or newspaper; string or wool; glue and brush; scissors.

Technique

Dragon   Cut out a long strip of material the same width as an egg carton and glue half egg cartons along it. At one end glue on a whole egg carton for the head and mouth as shown in Figure 1-37. Cut two large circles from cardboard and attach these to the sides of the head with glue to make the dragon's eyes. Decorate the egg carton dragon with thick green paint and allow it to dry.

Make a small hole through the upper sections of the dragon's mouth and three more at intervals along its body between the egg carton sections. Thread string through the holes and tie knots inside the mouth and under the material to keep the string in place. Hold the strings and make the puppet wriggle and bounce along.

Snake   Stuff a stocking with material scraps, old stockings, or rolled-up balls of newspaper and tie it at intervals along its length with scraps of wool to divide its body into a string of spheres. Tie lengths of string between some of the spheres and to the head, to control the puppet's movement when it is used. Glue material scraps onto the snake's body for decoration.

Both puppets can be more easily han-

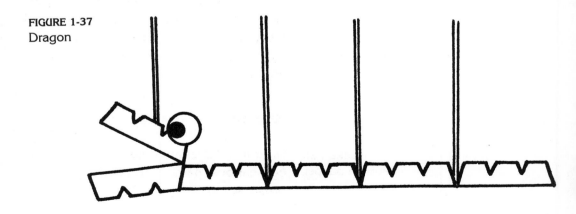

FIGURE 1-37
Dragon

dled by attaching the strings to two pieces of wood nailed together to make the handle shown in Figure 1-38. Drill holes at the ends of the wooden pieces, thread the strings through them, and tie knots to keep the strings in place.

Alternatively, tie the strings onto a wire coat hanger which has been bent into a square. The strings of the puppet are then attached to the corners of the wire square which is held horizontally and used to manipulate the puppet.

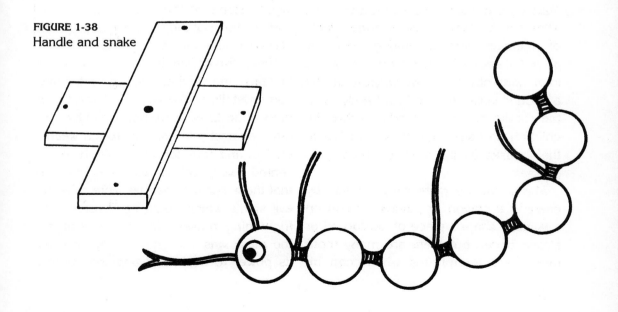

FIGURE 1-38
Handle and snake

Masks

Masks are fun to make and fun to wear. They can be made from a huge variety of materials, and decorating them will allow full scope for using junk-box items in all sorts of imaginative ways. It can be a good idea to have a mirror handy when the masks are being made so that the children can see what they look like in their masks as the work on them progresses.

Masks can be quite simply made by creating a crayon or painted design on a suitably shaped piece of cardboard or strong paper, but there are many more interesting techniques which can be used. Some of these are described in this section, but the children will probably discover others for themselves.

When the activity is introduced for the first time, the children may enjoy learning some details of the history of masks. In prehistoric times cavemen had little defense against wild animals, rough weather, fire, and thunder, all of which represented a very real danger. They believed that these natural enemies were ruled by evil spirits which could be resisted with frightening masks. The more terrifying the mask was, the greater they believed its power to be in resisting the enemy.

Masks have been, and still are, used all over the world on all sorts of occasions, including religious ceremonies, to chase away evil demons, in plays, and for decoration. In the classroom they can provide an excellent stimulus around which to develop a play or story.

MASKS FROM BAGS AND BOXES

Organization

When making masks the children should be encouraged to use all sorts of odds and ends from the junk boxes to decorate their masks and bring the flat, dull shapes of bags and boxes alive. Arrange the classroom or craft area so that the table for the group making masks is near the place where the junk is stored. Explain to the children that this technique is only safe with paper bags and not with plastic bags.

Materials

Large paper bags; cardboard boxes and cereal boxes; scissors; glue and brush; string; tape; junk-box scraps; material scraps; fur and leather scraps; water; crayons; paints and brush.

Technique

The bag or box mask is worn by placing the open end right over the head of the child. Large paper bags are suitable for face masks, and paper garment bags can be decorated and worn over the whole body, when holes are made for the arms to pass through. Cereal boxes might be large enough to pass over the head, but if not, use cardboard boxes or cartons with the back section cut away and attach strings through small holes on either side of the box to tie behind the head and keep the mask in position.

Place the bag or box over the head, and with the help of a partner, mark the positions of the eyes and mouth. Remove the bag or box and cut out shapes for the eyes and mouth. Decorate the surface of the mask to create an animal or character which can be real or imaginary.

Cat mask To make an animal mask such as the cat mask in Figure 2-3, the features of the animal should be exaggerated. Stiff material or paper can be used to make ears. Whiskers can be made from pipe cleaners pushed through holes in the bag. A scrap of fur can be glued onto the bag for the cat's nose. The whole mask can be decorated with paints or crayons.

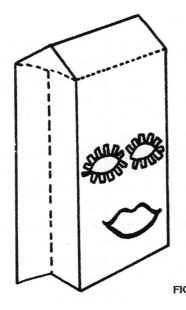

FIGURE 2-1
Basic bag shape for making a mask

FIGURE 2-2
Shapes for ears and nose—
curled paper makes good hair

FIGURE 2-3
Cat mask

FIGURE 2-1

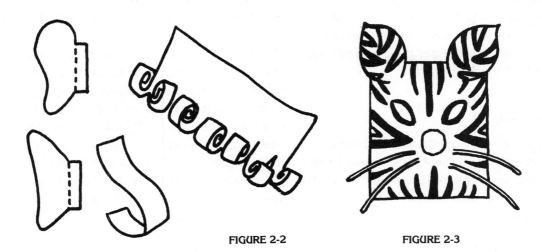

FIGURE 2-2   FIGURE 2-3

Space-creature mask For the space-creature mask shown in Figure 2-4, the basic shape is made from a cardboard box with the features glued onto it. Egg-carton sections can be used to make striking eyes, and a small box can be glued onto the big box for the nose. Pieces of wire with buttons attached to the ends create feelers for the mask when they are pushed through the box and secured in position with tape. The mouth of the space creature can be made by cutting out a shape from the cardboard box or by adding a mouth shape cut from material, polystyrene, or corrugated cardboard.

Glue all pieces of junk in place securely, but they must not be too heavy for the box to support. The masks can be further decorated with paints and crayons.

CONE AND CYLINDER MASKS

Organization

A large mask can be fun to make with someone else to share the problems and the work. One child can put the mask on, while the other observes and decides what further decoration is necessary.

Materials

Sheets of stiff cardboard; corrugated cardboard; scissors; glue and brush; junk-box scraps; cotton; Ping-Pong ball; paints and brush.

Technique

Both masks are worn right over the head and face so that the mask rests on the shoulders.

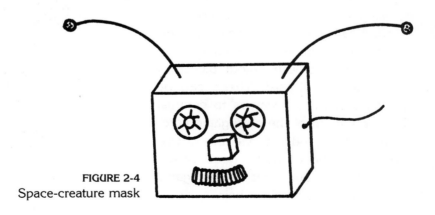

FIGURE 2-4
Space-creature mask

Cylinder mask Take a rectangular sheet of cardboard and roll it until it is big enough to pass over the child's head. Fasten the ends of the cardboard in position with staples, tape, or glue. Use a pencil to mark the position of the eyes, nose, and mouth. Stand the mask on a table and with a sharp pair of scissors cut out shapes for the eyes as shown in Figure 2-5. The three strips of paper hanging down are folded up to make eyelashes. Cut out a roughly triangular shape for the nose, leaving a small section at the top of the triangle attached to the cylinder as shown in Figure 2-5. The cut triangle is still attached to the mask and is folded down the center along the dotted line to make the nose. Teeth in the mouth can be cut out in the same way as the eyelashes. Hair can be made by cutting fancy shapes out of the top of the cylinder.

Masks can also be made in this way by using several thicknesses of corrugated cardboard rolled into a cylinder. Interesting effects can be made for features and decorations with cutout pieces of corrugated cardboard. These can be glued on in such a way as to contrast with the pattern of the corrugated cardboard of the cylinder. Small rolls of corrugated cardboard make good noses, and narrow cutout strips of corrugated cardboard make excellent hair.

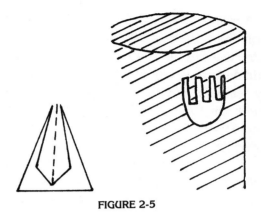

FIGURE 2-5

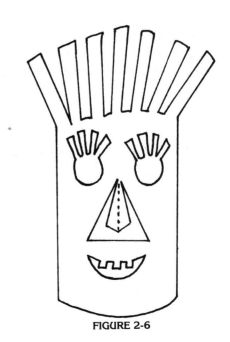

FIGURE 2-6

A cylinder mask decorated as a totem pole can be great fun to make and attractive to look at. A tall cylinder is used and decorated with toilet-paper rolls, boxes, feathers, and animals' heads cut from cardboard and glued onto the top. The whole mask is painted with bright colors when the structure is complete.

Santa Claus mask   Take a rectangular sheet of cardboard and roll it into a cone to fit the child's head. This is done by placing a finger about half way along the long side of the rectangle and, taking this to be the top point of the cone, rolling one of the corners nearest to this point down and inwards to make the cone as shown in Figure 2-7.

Using one hand to hold the point of the cone in position and the other hand to control the size of the rim, place the cone over the child's head and adjust the rim so that the cone passes comfortably over the child's head and rests on his or her shoulders. Staple the cardboard in position when the shape is right.

Mark and cut out holes for the eyes and mouth. Use scraps from the junk box to make the face. Santa Claus's eyebrows, moustache, beard, and hat trim are made from cotton or fur. His hat and cheeks are painted red, and a Ping-Pong ball is glued into position for his nose.

FIGURE 2-7

FIGURE 2-8
Santa Claus mask

PAPER-PLATE AND SHALLOW-CONE MASKS

Organization

Paper plates have many uses in craft work and should be included in the junk boxes. Encourage the children to bring in used but clean paper plates and cups left over from parties as they are too expensive to buy new except for very special projects.

Materials

Paper plates; fairly stiff cardboard; scissors; string; paints and brush; water; junk-box scraps; glue and brush.

Technique

Flower-face mask   Pierce two small holes on opposite sides of a paper plate near to the outside edge and use them to tie two lengths of string to the plate. These strings are tied at the back of the head to hold the mask in position. Use sharp scissors to cut out the eyes and mouth. Cut petal shapes from cardboard and glue these all around the edge of the plate at the back so that the glued areas are not visible.

Woodland-creature masks can be made by sticking leaves, twigs, and grasses onto the plate.

FIGURE 2-9
Flower-face mask

Shallow-cone masks A shallow cone is a useful base for decoration to make an animal mask. Cut a circle from a piece of cardboard that is of a suitable size to cover the face, or use a paper plate. Attach strings as before and cut out a section of the circle as shown in Figure 2-10. Bring the sides of the cut section together, overlap them slightly, and staple or glue them in this position. Decorate the mask, adding features with junk-box scraps or using paints.

A more pointed cone can be made by cutting a bigger section from a larger cardboard circle and joining the sides of the cut section together as before to make a shape suitable for decoration as a bird's head and beak or a horse's head.

FOLDED MASKS

Organization

The mask shown in Figure 2-11 is very simple to make and will require little explanation and guidance from the teacher. It is therefore a suitable technique for young children making their first mask. The mask shown in Figure 2-12 will involve drawing a pattern to be cut out from a folded sheet of cardboard. This pattern could be drawn by the teacher on the blackboard for older children to copy and draw on their cardboard. The children should be given the freedom to decorate the masks as they wish, as this will stimulate creativity.

FIGURE 2-10
Shallow-cone mask

FIGURE 2-11
Mask 1

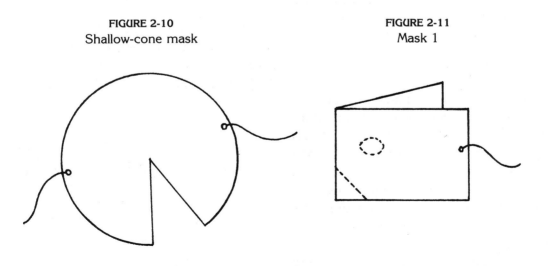

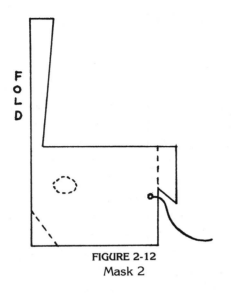

FIGURE 2-12
Mask 2

Materials

Sheets of fairly stiff cardboard; scissors; string; glue and brush; paints and brush; water; crayon; junk-box scraps.

Technique

Mask 1 The first mask is made by folding a rectangular sheet of cardboard in half and cutting away the areas shown by the dotted lines in Figure 2-11. Attach strings through small holes at each side to keep the mask in position on the face. Using this basic structure, decorate the mask, using paints, crayons, and junk-box scraps.

For an animal mask, cut out ears and glue them at the base inside the cardboard so that the glued area is hidden.

Mask 2 A folded mask with nose and ears can be made by cutting out the design shown in Figure 2-12 from a folded sheet of cardboard. Cut out the eye and nose sections as in the first mask. Attach strings on each side in the position shown. Open out the shape and bend forward the long vertical strip to make the nose. Gently reverse the fold which runs down the center of the nose section so that the fold points forward toward the front. Fold the ears along the dotted lines shown. Add further features and decorations if required. This technique can be used to create a striking, dramatic mask which the children will enjoy making and using.

Mask 3 The third type of folded mask is worn like a helmet, as shown in Figure 2-13. Cut out the shape shown in Figure 2-14 from a piece of folded cardboard.

Mask 3

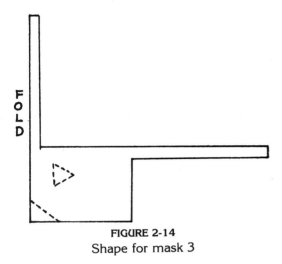

FIGURE 2-14
Shape for mask 3

Cut out holes for the eyes and open it out. Fold the vertical strip of cardboard back over the head to meet the horizontal strips which are joined together at the back of the head. Adjust the size of the helmet to fit the wearer and secure the cardboard strips in position with staples or glue. Decorate the masks with paints or junk-box scraps.

POLYSTYRENE STICK-MASKS

Organization

Before attempting this activity two essential pieces of equipment need to be bought: a polystyrene cutter with spare wires and a tube of polystyrene cement.

These can be obtained from hardware stores and stores that sell polystyrene tiles.

The teacher must demonstrate how to use the cutter before the children try to do so, and early attempts by the children should be closely supervised. The danger is that too much pressure will be applied to push the cutter through the polystyrene and the wire will snap.

Materials

Polystyrene tiles or large polystyrene meat dishes; polystyrene cutter; polystyrene cement.

Technique

Gently guide the polystyrene cutter through the polystyrene to cut the outer shape required for the mask. Cut out shapes from spare pieces of polystyrene to make the facial features. Stick these onto the mask with polystyrene cement. Use the cutter to cut out a stick of polystyrene of suitable thickness to support the mask. Use the polystyrene cement to attach the mask to the stick.

Polystyrene masks are rather limited in their structure and design, but the results can be exciting and original and the children will enjoy learning to use a new tool.

FIGURE 2-15
Polystyrene stick-mask

PAPIER-MÂCHÉ MASKS

Organization

Whenever papier-mâché is involved cover all table and immediate floor surfaces with newspaper. Make sure that the children's clothes are well protected with aprons and remind them to roll their sleeves up before they begin. Make sure that all dropped pieces of glued paper are retrieved and used so that cleaning up afterwards will be minimized.

Materials

Papier-mâché balloon masks Newspaper; balloon; cooking oil; bowl or bucket; powder and water paste (wallpaper paste is suitable); string; junk-box scraps; paints and brush; clear varnish.

Papier-mâché and clay or Plasticine masks Newspaper; cooking oil; bowl or bucket; craft knife or scissors; junk-box scraps; paints and brush; clear varnish.

Technique

Papier-mâché balloon masks Blow up a balloon and cover it with a thin layer of cooking oil. Make up the paste in a bucket and tear the newspaper into narrow strips. Dip the newspaper strips in the paste and cover the ballon with them. Continue in this way until about six layers of newspaper cover the balloon, leaving only the knot of the balloon uncovered by the papier-mâché. Smooth all over the surface by hand; then leave the newspaper to dry. When it is thoroughly dry, pop the balloon close to the knot so that only the papier-mâché shape remains. The covering of oil will allow the balloon to come away from the papier-mâché without difficulty. The papier-mâché balloon shape is then cut with a sharp knife or scissors in one of two ways. If it is cut down the dotted line as shown in Figure 2-16, two hollow oval shapes will be made, and each of these can be used to make a mask.

A mask made by cutting in this way is held in position by two strings which are tied at the back of the head. Make two small holes on each side of the mask with the point of the scissors. Thread a length of string through each hole and secure with a knot.

Use a sharp knife or scissors to cut out holes for the eyes, nose, and mouth. Papier-mâché features can be added by molding pieces of newspaper which have been soaked in the paste into suitable shapes. Attach the wet papier-mâché features by pressing them onto the mask and allowing them to dry. Alternatively, glue on egg-carton sections for the nose and eyes. Hair can be added by using wool, straw, frayed string, or strips of corrugated cardboard. When all the papier-mâché is dry the mask can be decorated with thick paints. A coat of clear varnish over the dried paint will complete the mask.

If the mask is cut as in Figure 2-17, it can be worn as a helmet with the upper section covering the top of the head. This mask can then be decorated in the same way as the first mask.

Papier-mâché and clay or Plasticine mask A realistic human face mask can be made with clay or Plasticine and papier-mâché. This technique is also suitable for animal and imaginary face masks.

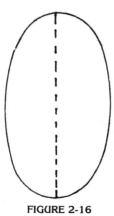

FIGURE 2-16

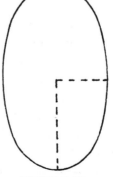

FIGURE 2-17

FIGURE 2-18

Mold a life-size face in clay or Plasticine on a board or tray as shown in Figure 2-18. Cover the face all over with a layer of oil. Dip strips of newspaper into the paste as described before and lay them carefully all over the surface of the clay or Plasticine, molding them to fit the contours of the face. Build up about six layers of papier-mâché in this way and leave them to dry. When the papier-mâché is thoroughly dry, carefully remove all the clay or Plasticine to leave the papier-mâché form of the face. Cut out shapes for the eyes, nostrils, and mouth and decorate as before. Attach a piece of elastic or string to the sides of the mask to hold the mask in position on the child's head.

The clay and Plasticine need not be wasted. If clay is used, the oil must be scraped off the surface and the clay left to soak in water until soft. Then it can be rolled into balls and saved.

The Plasticine can be rolled up and used again. If it has become very hard, it can be softened by immersing it in warm water for a while, drying it in a towel, and then kneading it with both hands.

Crayons

Crayons are possibly the most versatile and useful of drawing materials. They are convenient, readily available, and can be used on their own or in conjunction with a variety of other art materials to produce many different effects without the need for elaborate equipment.

Many of the techniques described in this section require materials that will already be available in the classroom, so little preparation will be necessary for these activities. The basic requirements are a variety of papers on which to use the crayons and the crayons themselves. The selection of papers should include some good-quality cartridge paper and also some thinner paper for more detailed work.

For some techniques, other easily available tools will be necessary. A variety of scraping tools could include old ballpoint pens, blunt knives, cocktail sticks, combs, broken linoleum cutters, and steel wool. Watercolor and a soft paintbrush will be needed for wax resist and batik effects. Cooking oil is used to make transparent pictures; small quantities of oil could be supplied by the children and poured into a communal jug or bowl to be shared by them all. Plaster of Paris has many uses in school and may be available from the school stores. If not, it can be bought from craft shops or from large pharmacies where it is sold as dental plaster. It will be needed for taking rubbings from a plaster block.

But, a word of warning. Fragments of crayon worked into tables and floors by feet and hands are extremely difficult to remove. It is therefore a good idea to cover all work surfaces and even the floor with newspaper when crayons are used. It will be well worth the time and trouble saved by not having to remove stubborn stains, and it will also help to keep the good will of the classroom custodian!

BULL'S-EYE PATTERNS

Organization

This activity is suitable for a class lesson as the materials required are very simple and a display of a large number of these designs is most effective. Mount the patterns side by side in blocks or panels. All work surfaces should be protected with sheets of newspaper.

Materials

Small sheets of cartridge paper; wax crayons; large sheet of paper for mounting the patterns.

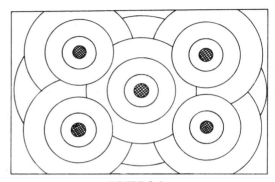

FIGURE 3-1
Bull's-eye patterns

Technique

Draw five small circles on the sheet of cartridge paper in a pattern as shown in Figure 3-1 by the shaded areas. Fill in the circles with very thickly applied wax crayon. Use different colors to draw rings around each of the small circles and color in the spaces between consecutive rings. Continue in this way until the whole page is covered, repeating the pattern even when complete circles cannot be drawn.

CRAYON SGRAFFITO

Organization

When experimenting with sgraffito, care needs to be taken to protect work surfaces from fragments of crayon. For early

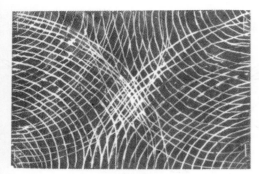

FIGURE 3-2
Crayon sgraffito

experiments it is safer for the children to use coins, nails, and pen nibs rather than scissors or knives.

Materials

Sheets of paper; wax crayons; tools for scraping such as coins, nails, pen nibs, nail files, and hacksaw blades.

Technique

Apply a thick layer of light-colored crayon to a sheet of paper. Cover this with a second layer of crayon, using a darker shade or several colors. Make a design by carefully scratching away the top surface of crayon to reveal the colors underneath.

Various effects can be achieved by experimenting with different tools.

CUT-CRAYON PATTERNS

Organization

This is an activity suitable for a group of children because a collection of grooved crayons of different colors can be made and shared by the whole group. The teacher should supervise the cutting of the crayons with younger children. Ensure that the work surfaces are covered as small pieces of crayon are extremely difficult to remove when they have been pressed into the table or floor.

Materials

Crayons; scissors or knives (not too sharp); papers of different colors and textures.

Technique

Using a knife or one blade of a pair of scissors, carefully cut grooves into the side of a crayon. Rub the grooved edge

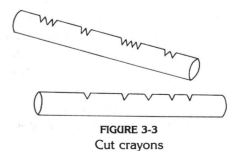

FIGURE 3-3
Cut crayons

48

on the paper, using straight and curved lines to create the best effect. Overlap the patterns with grooved crayon lines in different colors or apply the colors in separate areas, using lines, blocks, and curves.

RESIST PATTERNS AND PICTURES

Organization

This technique is suitable for a group of children working together on a large-scale picture such as a Halloween scene or an underwater design. It is a good idea for the children to work on the floor. The completed pictures should be dried flat.

Materials

Large sheet of paper; candle or wax crayons; watercolors; soft brush.

Technique

Make a bold drawing using a candle or light-colored wax crayons. Lightly brush a wash of dark watercolor all over the surface of the picture with a soft paintbrush. The crayon design should be thick enough to show through the wash of color. The original drawing or pattern will

FIGURE 3-4
Resist picture

remain largely uncovered by the paint. Experiment by developing the picture in stages, allowing each wash to dry before applying further designs using more wax and more paint and by selecting different areas of the picture for treatment. Alternatively, divide the pages into sections and complete each section separately using crayons and paints of different colors.

Washes of paint can also be applied to crayon rubbings, transfers, and sgraffito pictures for a similar effect.

TRANSPARENT PICTURES

Organization

When working on transparent pictures, a bowl of oil can be shared by several children working on one large surface, such as the floor or a group of tables pushed together. The pictures are most effective when mounted on windows so that the light shines through them.

Materials

Large sheet of cartridge paper; wax crayons; a clean cloth; vegetable oil; black paper for the frame; scissors; glue and brush.

Technique

Using wax crayons, draw a design on a sheet of cartridge paper. Include some broad areas of color as well as lines. Then rub vegetable oil lightly over the back with a clean cloth. The picture can then be seen from both sides like a stained-glass window.

Glue a strip of black paper all around the edge of the picture to frame it. Mount the work against a window so that the light shines through. In Figure 3-5, bold black lines have been used to make a striking stained-glass-window design. These lines can be left opaque or treated on the back with the oil to make them transparent. The spaces between the lines are filled in with color, using wax crayons. The picture is framed with a strip of black paper.

FIGURE 3-5
Transparent picture

TRANSFERS

Organization

It is often a good idea to introduce two similar techniques at the beginning of the lesson, so that the children can choose which they prefer. If the whole class or a large group of children are to participate in the activity, it can be convenient to place the necessary materials on tables around the room in order to avoid congestion.

Materials

A variety of papers: some thick, some thin, construction paper, tinted papers; wax crayons; chalks; pencils; ballpoint pens or wooden meat skewers.

FIGURE 3-6
Crayon and chalk transfer

Technique

Crayon transfers   Cover a page of thin paper with a thick layer of crayon and lay the page face down on a clean sheet of paper. Draw on the top surface with a ballpoint pen, pencil, or wooden meat skewer. When the pages are separated, two designs will be revealed.

Crayon and chalk transfers   Apply chalk to a sheet of coarse-grained paper such as construction paper. Use fingers to rub the chalk well into the grain of the paper and shake the page to remove any excess powdered chalk.

Apply a thick layer of wax crayon all over the chalky surface of the paper. Place a sheet of paper on top of the chalk and wax surface and make a design on the top page with a ballpoint pen, pencil, or meat skewer as shown in Figure 3-6. Separate the pages. The top page will pick up a chalk- and crayon-textured design and the lower page will have the same design in reverse. Colored chalks and tinted papers will give even more interesting effects.

CRAYON BATIK

Organization

This activity involves soaking the page in water and then allowing it to dry. For this reason, the group should work near a sink and have access to a table where the wet pages can be left to dry flat.

Materials

Sheets of fairly thin, good-quality paper; wax crayons; a bowl of water; paints or ink; a large, fairly soft brush.

Technique

Using thick wax crayons make a design on the paper. Crumple the paper into a

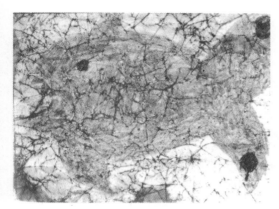

FIGURE 3-7
Crayon batik

ball and immerse it in a bowl of water. Remove it from the water and carefully open out the sheet of paper and place it on several layers of newspaper. Apply a wash of dark paint or ink to the whole page. The paint will penetrate the cracks in the wax design to give a batik effect. When dry, the wax colors can be polished by rubbing lightly with a soft cloth.

This technique gives added interest to leaf, butterfly, and fish designs which can be included in a frieze or collage.

SIMPLE RUBBINGS

Organization

This activity can be enjoyed in the classroom, the playground, a park, or in the street. As long as they are working in a safe place, large numbers of children can participate in the activity.

Materials

Sheets of thin paper; wax crayons; a variety of objects to be rubbed such as coins, string, textured wallpapers, cog wheels, bricks, license plates, wheels, tombstones, bark, leaves, and feathers.

Technique

Lay a sheet of paper over the object selected for rubbing. Take an impression of its embossed surface by gently rubbing over the paper with the side of an unwrapped crayon. Experiment with different colored crayons and tinted papers.

FIGURE 3-8
Rubbing of a Brighton coal hole

Gold and silver crayons can be particularly effective and are exciting to use. Texture and interest can be added to collage pictures by cutting out rubbed designs and including them in the picture.

RUBBINGS FROM YOUR OWN DESIGN

Organization

The children can make their own designs for rubbing or they can work in a group to make one large design which can be rubbed with different colored crayons.

Materials

Sheet of strong backing paper or cardboard; scissors; glue and brush; cardboard; dried leaves; feathers; material; wallpaper; leather; sandpaper; corrugated cardboard; string or raffia; wax crayons; paper.

Technique

Cut out shapes from a variety of textured surfaces, such as the ones suggested above, and arrange them on a sheet of paper or cardboard. Glue them onto the paper securely, and when the glue is dry, place a sheet of paper on top of the embossed design and rub carefully over the surface with crayon.

Alternatively, make a design by gluing a length of string or raffia onto the cardboard, and when the glue is dry, lay a sheet of paper on top and take rubbings with the wax crayon.

A different kind of picture can be made by cutting out recognizable shapes of animals, people, buildings, etc., gluing them onto stiffer backing paper, and then taking rubbings from these in the same way.

A long repeat pattern can be made by unwinding a roll of plain paper and taking rubbings at intervals along its length.

The design can be used as wallpaper in the classroom or as a background for display purposes.

FIGURE 3-9
Rubbing from cut card

RUBBINGS FROM A PLASTER BLOCK

Organization

The use of plaster of Paris must be carefully supervised. It must be mixed quickly and to the right consistency. It is also important that any surplus is disposed of correctly. It must never be poured down the sink as it may set there and block the drain.

Materials

A bowl; stick for mixing; water; plaster of Paris (this can be bought from a pharmacy as dental plaster); polystyrene dish; small stick, knife or clay modeling tool; thin paper; wax crayons.

Technique

Prepare a small quantity of plaster of Paris by sifting the powder through your fingers as you sprinkle it slowly and evenly onto the water. A mixture of approximately 14 ounces (400 grams) of powder to three-quarters of a pint (0.3 liters) of water is correct. When small islands of dry plaster start to form on the surface, leave the mixture for one minute; then use a stick to mix it to the right consistency for use. It is important that

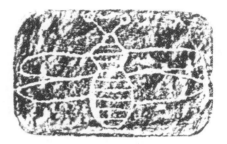
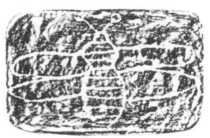

FIGURE 3-10
Rubbing from a plaster block

the whole procedure be done quickly because setting starts as soon as the powder gets wet and is complete in about ten minutes.

Pour the plaster of Paris into a polystyrene dish. After a minute or two, while the plaster of Paris is still damp, draw a design in the plaster with a stick, knife, or clay modeling tool. Leave it for a few minutes to allow the plaster to set. When it has hardened, lay a sheet of paper on top and rub with a crayon over the surface to make an impression of the design.

Picture Making

In this section I have included any techniques for making pictures that do not fall easily into any of the other categories in this book. Many of the techniques described are extremely simple and require very little preparation or planning by the teacher. They are activities suitable for young children learning basic skills and also for older children who will enjoy developing a simple idea and exploiting its possibilities.

The children will respond enthusiastically to these ideas for creative work if they are suggested by an interested and encouraging teacher. The attitude of the teacher toward the work that he or she is suggesting is always very important. If he or she believes an activity will prove interesting and give good results, this is likely to happen. The teacher's job is to stimulate, encourage, and reward with praise so that the children will gain confidence and enjoy developing their creative skills to the fullest.

MOSAIC AND COLOR-TONE PICTURES

Organization

This activity will involve painting a large sheet of paper which is to be cut into small squares. Before the paper is cut into squares, the paint must be allowed to dry completely. There may be enough space in the classroom or activity area to dry the paper flat, but if not, tie some string clotheslines across the windows or walls and use clothespins to hang the paintings out of the way while they are drying.

Materials

Painting paper; paints and brush; scissors; paste and brush; cartridge paper.

Technique

Fold a sheet of painting paper in half. Continue folding in half until the folded paper is about the same size as a postcard. Open it out and paint each folded section in either different colors or different tones of one color. When the paint is dry, cut out each of the sections and cut them into small squares about three-quarters of an inch (two centimeters) square.

Mosaic pictures Use the cut-out squares to build up a mosaic picture by pasting them close together onto a sheet of cartridge paper to make a picture or abstract design.

Color-tone mosaic A color-tone picture can be made to illustrate different tones of one color. Paste some of the

FIGURE 4-1
Color-tone picture

darker colored cutout squares at the center of a piece of cartridge paper, grouping them closely together in a fairly random arrangement. Now stick some squares of a lighter tone of the same color all around the outside of the darker squares. Continue in this way so that the picture is built up with dark tones of color at the center of the design progressing to light tones of the same color at the edges.

DOODLE LINES

Organization

The spaces made by the lines in this picture can be filled with interesting materials, such as dried seeds, beans, and rice. Sort these into groups by color and

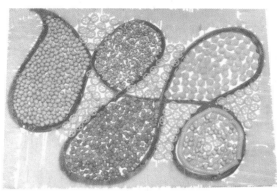

FIGURE 4-2
Doodle lines filled in,
using collage technique

size and put them in polystyrene trays. This will make selection much easier because the children will not have to sort through all the junk boxes for these materials when they are required.

Materials

Paper; paints and brush; dried seeds; beans; colored aquarium gravel; dyed rice; painted eggshells; tissue paper; glue and brush.

Technique

Use a brush heavily charged with black or any dark-colored paint to make a random line design on the paper. Use curves, straight lines, and angles to make an interesting pattern. Allow the painted lines to dry; then fill in the spaces between the lines with colored paints. Alternatively, use a collage technique and fill in the spaces with rice, aquarium gravel, or painted pieces of eggshell. Small scraps of tissue paper can be rolled tightly into little balls and glued onto the paper. These can be packed closely together to make blocks of color.

The spaces may be filled in by a combination of painting and collage techniques in the same picture to create exciting effects.

For the purely painted design, a cheap painting paper may be used, but for the collage technique a thicker, better-quality paper will be necessary.

GRAINING AND STIPPLING

Organization

Graining and stippling can be particularly suitable for a group of children as they can share the box of tools for making the patterns. Learning to share materials and working happily with others are an important part of a child's education, and art and craft activities provide excellent practice in this.

Materials

Fairly thick paper; paints and brush; flour; water; jug; comb; cardboard; rag.

Technique

Use a paintbrush to mix flour and water in a jug to make a smooth, thick paste and add some powder paint to color it. Use the brush to apply the colored paste to a whole sheet of thick paper. Use the teeth of a comb or the serrated edge of a piece of stiff cardboard cut from the side of a cardboard box to make patterns in the paste. Draw the comb through the paste, using lines and curves to create interesting effects. Experiment with different tools to make patterns in the paste. Some tools worth trying are rags, stiff brushes, cocktail or popsicle sticks, and straws. Encourage the children to make their own tools for scraping from polystyrene, plastic containers, and thick leaves such as holly.

If desired, prints can be taken from the picture while it is still wet by laying a clean sheet of paper on top of the design and applying gentle pressure all over the page to take the print.

FIGURE 4-3
Graining and stippling

PICTURES USING BLEACH

Organization

Take great care when the children use bleach so that none is spilled on clothes or furniture, as the effects can be disastrous—bleach will remove color from most materials. Techniques involving the use of bleach should only be attempted by older children. The teacher must ensure that the children know that bleach is poisonous and that they must wash their hands after using it.

Materials

Paper; paints or ink and brush; matchstick; small pot of bleach.

Technique

Apply a wash of paint or ink to the whole sheet of paper and allow it to dry. Dip a matchstick into a pot of bleach and draw a design with it on the painted or inked surface, using lines, curves, and blobs. To bleach larger areas of the paper, use a brush dipped in bleach. A contrasting pattern will emerge whenever the bleach is applied to the painted or inked surface of the paper. The technique is particularly useful where a dark background to a picture is required, as with pictures depicting a night-time scene such as fireworks on the Fourth of July.

FIGURE 4-4
Bleach picture

NUMBER PICTURES

Organization

Many children have difficulty learning to write numbers correctly. However, they will enjoy painting number pictures, and if the pictures are displayed so that they can be seen when the children are doing arithmetic, the paintings will serve as a constant reminder to them of how to form the numbers correctly.

Materials

Paper; paints and brush.

Technique

Use a thick brush with paint to paint a big number on a sheet of paper. Choose another color and paint around the outline of the first number. Continue in this way, repeating the number on both sides of the original figure. When it is no longer

FIGURE 4-5
Number picture

possible to paint whole numbers on the page, fill in the remaining spaces with bands of color, as shown in Figure 4-5. Number pictures in the sequence 1 to 10 are often effective when mounted as a frieze.

GRADED-SIZE PICTURES AND SPREAD-OUT SHAPES

Organization

Both these pictures involve cutting out paper shapes and sticking them onto paper. Graded-size pictures may appeal more to younger or less skilled children and can be used to illustrate rhymes and stories such as "Goldilocks and the Three Bears." These pictures are also a good exercise in grading and sorting for young children.

The technique of spreading out a shape to make an interesting picture requires inventiveness and can be a more stimulating activity for older children.

Materials

Tissue paper; black paper; scissors; paste and brush.

Technique

Graded-size pictures Cut out a sequence of shapes from black paper. These could illustrate the themes of small to large, possibly relating to the members of a family, or thin to fat shapes to tell the story of a greedy animal. Paste the shapes onto a sheet of tissue paper in order of size.

Display the picture against the light for the maximum effect. The tissue paper can be attached to the window frame with transparent tape or stuck directly onto the glass with small balls of putty-like adhesive available from a stationery store.

Spread-out shapes Cut out a regular or irregular shape from a piece of black paper. Cut the whole of it into pieces. Arrange all of these pieces on a sheet of tissue paper. The design can be a carefully ordered sequence of shapes cut from the original shape or it can be a collection of small cut pieces arranged to make a completely different design. Experiment with several arrangements before pasting them in position. Allow the paste to dry; then display the picture

FIGURE 4-6
Spread-out shape made from
circle cut into sections

against the light on a window, so that the dark paper shapes show up clearly against the contrasting color of the tissue paper, through which the light will shine.

PAPER RELIEF PICTURES

Organization

It is dangerous to store glue and paint in glass containers—large yogurt cartons or squat plastic bowls are much more suitable. Washed stones or pebbles can be put at the base of lightweight containers to make them more stable.

Materials

Fairly strong backing paper or thinner paper pasted onto cardboard; cartridge paper; toilet-paper rolls; boxes; glue and brush.

Technique

A variety of paper shapes are glued onto a sheet of paper to make an original design. Toilet-paper rolls can be cut into rings and glued onto the paper to make the picture in Figure 4-7. Designs can also be made by using boxes of different shapes and colors. Try cutting slits in the

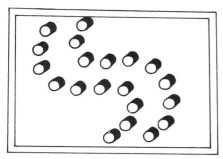

FIGURE 4-7
Paper relief picture

backing paper and weaving strips of paper in and out of them to create loops.

Pieces of paper can be used in many ways to make relief pictures. The paper can be cut and folded to make spirals, cones, pleats, and curls.

To make paper curl, place a strip of paper flat against the blade of a pair of scissors and close the blades without cutting the paper. Carefully pull the paper strip out and over the back of the blade as shown in Figure 4-8.

FIGURE 4-8

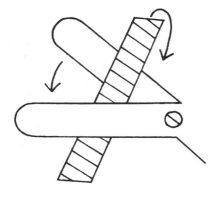

CHESSBOARD PATTERNS AND PAPER WEAVING

Organization

For these activities it is not necessary to use conventional art and craft papers. Experiment with plain and patterned paper bags, wrapping paper, tin-can labels, and aluminum foil. Making simple chessboard-pattern pictures is a suitable activity for young children who will enjoy the pattern's regular design and bold effect.

Materials

Paper; paints and brush; gummed colored paper; scissors; paste and brush; cardboard; colored paper bags; wrapping paper; tin-can labels; aluminum foil.

Technique

Chessboard-pattern pictures Fold a square sheet of paper in half and then in quarters. Continue folding the paper in this way until regular squares of a suitable size are made by the folds when the paper is opened out.

Open the page out and paint alternate squares in one or more bright colors.

Another way of making a chessboard pattern is with pieces of gummed colored paper, or one of the types of paper suggested above, stuck onto alternate squares made by the folds on the sheet of paper.

Paper weaving   With this technique strips of paper are threaded horizontally in and out of vertical slits cut in a piece of paper.

First, a sheet of paper is cut to make a loom on which the horizontal strips will be woven. To make the loom, fold a piece of paper in half and cut slits from the fold up to within about three-quarters of an inch (two centimeters) of the top. Unfold this loom and weave horizontal strips of paper in and out of the vertical slits which have just been made. Chess-board patterns are made by weaving the paper in the usual regular pattern. Alternatively, a less regular pattern can be made by varying the spaces between the slits when cutting the loom. It is also possible to make interesting irregular patterns by not weaving the paper under each slit or by weaving it over more than one slit. Further effects can be created by weaving several different colored and textured paper strips through the slits on the loom.

Another method of paper weaving is to cut zigzag lines through the folded paper when making the loom, as shown in Figure 4-9. Vary the width of the paper strips used on this loom and avoid weaving them too regularly.

FIGURE 4-9
Paper-weaving loom with zigzag lines

FIGURE 4-10
Strips of paper of varying widths
woven through the loom

FIGURE 4-11
Paper weaving

Designs can also be made on a non-folded paper loom so that asymmetrical patterns are created. Cut wavy slits in a large piece of paper and weave strips of paper through these.

DRAWINGS FROM LIFE

Organization

When making drawings from life, the children will enjoy sitting in a circle around the subject, and the result will be an interesting collection of pictures of the same subject seen from different angles. Drawings of this kind will teach observation and encourage concentration.

Materials

Paper, plain white or tinted; pencils or charcoal; very large sheet of paper; paints and brush; crayons.

Technique

Two different techniques are described here for drawing people.

For the first technique, sit the children

in a circle around the subject. They can sit at desks or balance their drawing paper on books or boards on their laps. Arrange the human subject in some interesting way, preferably sitting, so that the person will be able to maintain the position for quite a long time if necessary. Ask the children to observe carefully and record in their drawings of the subject details such as hair texture, shape of the face and features, and so on. This can be done with a still-life group, a pet, or a human subject.

For the second technique of drawing people, a child lies down on a large sheet of paper or several small pieces of paper glued together and another child draws around him. When the outline of the child is complete, the details of the figure are filled in with crayons or paint.

This technique is suitable for making figures for large-scale friezes. The children will enjoy the novelty of drawing life-size pictures of people.

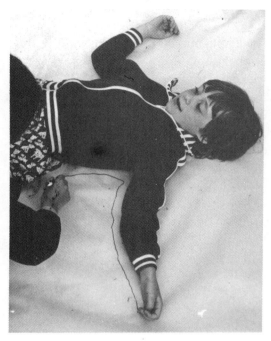

FIGURE 4-12
Drawings from life—second technique

plete the design in one session; then organization of space and materials is kept to a minimum and the children are able to reach a satisfying conclusion to their work when the picture is completed without long, enforced breaks.

JUNK MONSTER

Organization

A junk relief picture is best made on a large scale by a group of children working together. Organize the day so that the children have the opportunity to com-

Materials

Cardboard; pencil; cardboard egg cartons; glue and brush; scissors; paints and brush; odds and ends from the junk boxes.

Technique

A suitable subject for a junk relief picture is an imaginary monster or dragon. To make the dragon, lightly sketch its outline in pencil on a large sheet of strong cardboard or paper. Cut paper egg cartons in half and glue the protruding sections of the egg carton onto the dragon to create a three-dimensional effect. Fill in the whole of the dragon's body, head, and tail in this way, cutting out smaller sections of egg cartons where necessary. Paint in the dragon's legs and feet and add any other odds and ends from the junk boxes to decorate him if required.

These could include buttons for eyes and cotton to represent smoke from his nostrils. When the glue has dried and the egg cartons are firmly in position, cover the dragon with thick green paint and fill in any background details which are required, using paints or any collage or printing techniques desired.

CONCERTINA CUTOUTS

Organization

Cutout designs are interesting in themselves or they can be incorporated in a

FIGURE 4-13
Junk monster

larger picture or illustration. They can be used to illustrate lines of trees, rows of houses, groups of people, and so on.

They are also useful when making a frieze to illustrate a rhyme or a song such as "Mary Had a Little Lamb" or "The Twelve Days of Christmas."

Materials

Paper or thin cardboard; scissors; paints and brush; crayons; felt-tip pens.

Technique

Fold a long strip of paper into a concertina shape as shown in Figure 4-14. Fold the concertina flat and lightly sketch the shape of a person, tree, duck, or other subject on the front, as shown in Figure 4-15. It is essential that the shape should reach from one side of the paper to the other so that the concertina is held together when it is unfolded. Cut out the design, remembering not to cut the hinges which join the shapes together.

Open it out and decorate the row of shapes with paints, crayons, or felt-tip pens.

The pattern could be displayed standing loosely folded in the concertina shape or stuck onto a sheet of contrasting colored backing paper. It can also be used as part of a larger illustration.

Original party invitations can be made from a cutout row of children, birthday cakes, or balloons. Details of the party, such as time, place, and occasion, can be written on the sections.

FIGURE 4-14

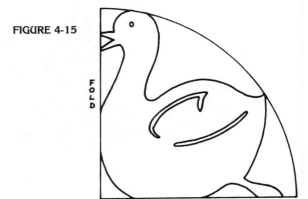

FIGURE 4-15

FOLD

FOLD

Cutout paper designs can also be made from squares or circles folded into quarters. The shape to be cut out is drawn on the folded paper quarter as described before. To hold the design together when the shape is opened out, the subject should include one or more parts of all the sides of the folded paper quarter. Figure 4-15 shows a suitable design drawn on a folded circle of paper.

Collage

Collage is a word derived from the French verb *coller,* which means to paste or stick. A collage is an arrangement of several different shapes, cut or torn from various materials, which form a pleasing combination of shapes, textures, and colors when glued onto a sheet of paper to make a permanent picture. I have also included in this section the techniques of montage and photomontage.

All the methods for making pictures described in this section are simple and suitable for children of all ages. The materials used are cheap and easily available. Many of them will already be stored in the junk-box corner in the classroom

if it is organized as described in Chapter 6.

Sufficient newspaper, magazines, and postcards can easily be accumulated for collage, montage, and photomontage work by asking the children to bring one or two of each with them when they come to school. Old wallpaper catalogs will provide another source of material. The children will enjoy using the sheets of brightly colored, patterned, and textured papers.

There are many ways of making collage pictures. Some are included in this section, but if allowed freedom to experiment, the children will discover many more. They should always be encouraged to try out their own ideas and experiment with their own variations on a particular theme.

SILHOUETTE PICTURES

Organization

This simple technique can be used to create individual pictures by each child, or a large-scale picture can be made by a group of children working together.

Materials

White cartridge paper on which to mount the design; sheets of colored paper; paste and brush; scissors.

Technique

The shapes for the silhouette picture or pattern are cut or torn from the sheets of colored paper and pasted onto the cartridge paper. The shapes should be bold and simple. The children should be encouraged not to paste the pieces onto the design too soon; they should first work out roughly what the final arrangement will be.

Cut shapes are suitable for subjects with a clearly defined outline, such as ships, houses, churches, steeples, and castles. Torn shapes are good for representing subjects with less clearly defined outlines, such as clouds, smoke, waves, and hair.

Suitable subjects for silhouette collages are geometric patterns, portraits (profiles), jazz bands, aquariums, animals, and landscape.

COLORED-TISSUE MONTAGE

Organization

It is sometimes necessary to restrict the amount of tissue paper used as children can be very wasteful and resources are

FIGURE 5-1
Elephant silhouettes

FIGURE 5-2
Colored-
tissue
montage

paper. It is often easier, however, to paste the paper on which the design is to be mounted and lay the torn tissue-paper shapes on top of this. A thin layer of paste can then be applied on top of the tissue-paper shapes. When making the shapes, the children should not use scissors, nor should they draw the picture on the tissue paper before tearing, as both tend to spoil the spontaneous effect of the design. Overprint effects can be made by overlapping the tissue shapes in the picture; for example, orange is made if yellow is pasted over red. Many shades of one color can be obtained by using this method.

This technique can be used to create effects of sky, hills, or sea to use as a background for other pictures or models.

Tissue-paper colors fade quickly. For more permanence, tint the tissue paper with watercolors or acrylic paints before or after pasting.

often limited. A cardboard box should be placed near the children who are making the pictures to be used as a communal store for leftover scraps of tissue which can then be used by others. In this way, each child can start with one colored sheet of tissue paper and build up his or her picture by using other colors of tissue taken from the communal store.

Materials

Colored tissue paper; paste and brush; white cartridge paper.

Technique

The picture is made by pasting torn tissue-paper shapes onto the cartridge

RECESSION PICTURES

Organization

An introductory discussion will help to explain recession and how it is obtained by placing light colors in the background and dark shades in the foreground.

Materials

A wide selection of colors of tinted pastel paper; paste and brush; scissors; stiff backing paper; pen and ink.

Technique

Using the subject of a city skyline as an example, the children begin by cutting a number of dramatic skylines, including towers, chimneys, domes, and cranes, from the tinted pastel paper. The skylines are pasted on the backing paper, starting with the lightest tint at the top of the paper to suggest the far distance, and working forward to the darkest shade to suggest the near foreground.

FIGURE 5-3

Buildings in the foreground can be more clearly defined and decorated with pen and ink.

Subjects suitable for this type of exercise are fairground scenes, shipbuilding yards, industrial landscapes, and city skylines.

WALLPAPER PICTURES

Organization

Outdated wallpaper catalogs can easily be obtained from decorating shops at a low price or free of charge (the children may know someone who works in a shop of this kind who will be able to obtain catalogs). Excellent materials for artwork are often obtained through contacts of the children. As the children become accustomed to bringing useful things into school for artwork an interesting collection will gradually be built up. Never assume that it is the teacher who must collect and provide all the materials. Many of the children will take pride in bringing the largest quantity or the most interesting collection into school.

Materials

Patterned wallpaper; paste and brush; fairly stiff cartridge paper; scissors.

Technique

The children should enjoy leafing through the pages of the wallpaper catalog and will often be inspired to create pictures and patterns with them. Some abstract patterns may suggest sea life, flowers, birds, and zoo animals to the children.

The shapes of the subject are cut from the wallpaper and arranged, before pasting, on the cartridge paper. When a satisfactory arrangement has been found, the shapes are pasted down.

Patchwork patterns are easily made by cutting out hexagons, squares, or triangles of the same size and pasting them down side by side to create a patchwork effect shown in Figure 5-4.

FIGURE 5-4
Wallpaper picture

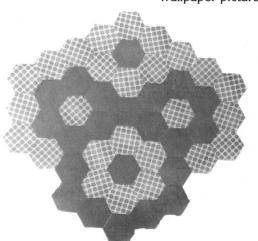

NEWSPAPER, MAGAZINE, AND PAPER MONTAGE

Organization

This can be a fairly spontaneous activity, where the children use cuttings from newspapers and magazines already in the classroom, or it can be the culmination of collecting articles from the paper on a topical subject, such as the Olympic Games or a long yacht race.

Materials

Newspapers and magazines; paste and brush; scissors; poster colors; water; paints and brush; white cartridge paper.

Technique

Newspaper and magazine collage can be used in many ways. It can illustrate a subject or theme related to topic work or something controversial, such as pollution. All newspaper cuttings on the subject are cut out, collected, and finally arranged carefully and stuck onto the cartridge paper. Pictures should be included as well as written articles and headlines. Words can be made from individual letters cut out from the paper or magazine.

Events such as the children's vacations

FIGURE 5-5

a sheet of cartridge paper. Some of the advertisements can be torn to suggest old and weathered posters. When the pieces have been pasted and pressed firmly down, the foreground is painted on top.

Other useful scraps which might be included in pictures of this kind are confetti, sandpaper, greeting cards, artificial flowers, playing cards, jar and can labels, stamps, photos, and used cigarette and candy wrappers.

PHOTO MONTAGE

Organization

Planning and constructing a photo montage can be an excellent cooperative exercise for several children who want to work together, as well as for the individual child. Group work encourages the children to share materials as well as ideas.

can be illustrated by newspaper collage pictures, such as advertisements for the holiday resort, photographs of people on the beach and in traffic jams, cuttings from local papers, and so on. The collage can be further developed by adding other souvenirs of the vacation, such as postcards, sections of maps, tickets, and photographs.

Newspaper collage can also be used as the background to a picture, suggesting walls and advertising billboards where posters are displayed. The children cut a number of advertisements from a newspaper or magazine and paste them onto

Materials

Magazine photographs; picture postcards; paste and brush; scissors; cartridge paper.

Technique

First a study of the available material is made so that a picture theme can be decided upon. When this has been done, the outlines of the picture are roughly drawn on the cartridge paper with a soft pencil so that the main areas are clearly defined. The children select and cut out the pieces of the photographs that they require for their pictures, and then arrange them on the paper and paste them down to make a permanent picture. Figure 5-6 shows how successfully sections of photographs can be used to make an interesting picture.

FIGURE 5-6

STRING PICTURES

Organization

A box containing long and short pieces of string, twine, yarn, wool, ribbon, and raffia, left over from previous activities, is a valuable addition to the junk-box collection.

Materials

Thin cardboard; pencil; a variety of pieces of string, twine, yarn, and similar materials; scissors; glue and brush; paints and brush.

Technique

Lightly sketch a design in pencil on a sheet of cardboard. Suitable themes for string pictures are birds, trees, flowers, and animals. Apply a fairly thick layer of glue to one part of the picture, either to a complete shape, such as a bird or flower, or a section of a larger shape,

FIGURE 5-7
String picture

and lay a piece of string all around the edge of it. Lay a second piece of string, twine, yarn, or wool next to the first piece and press it down lightly to secure it in position. Use string or some of the other materials suggested above to fill in all the glued area with curves and straight lines.

Apply glue to another section of the design and repeat the technique. Continue in this way until the picture is complete.

FIGURE 5-8
String picture

If required, paint a background in a color which blends in with the colors already used for the design, or cut the design out and mount it on a separate sheet of paper.

Rubbings can be taken from string pictures by using wax crayons and paper, as previously described.

RELIEF COLLAGE FROM JUNK

Organization

Collage pictures are very effective when they are made on a large scale. They are therefore ideally suited to group work. The children can work with the backing paper hung up on the wall where it will be displayed when the picture is complete. They can assemble the picture standing on low tables pushed against the wall if the paper is too high for them to reach from the floor. By doing this, they are able to stand back from the picture from time to time to get an impression of the effects they are creating and what the end result will be.

Materials

A strong backing sheet on which to paste the design (the plain white back of an old poster is ideal for mounting lighter objects; cardboard cut from the side of a large cardboard box is suitable for mounting a display of heavier objects); paper scraps; a wide variety of materials from the junk box; paste and brush; scissors.

Technique

The basic plan of the picture is decided upon and the picture is built up by using items from the junk boxes. The background to the picture can be painted beforehand if required.

The steam engine shown in Figure 5-9 is a relief collage of fabric, cotton, paper, cardboard, and sand. The engine

FIGURE 5-9
Relief collage

of the train is made from a piece of corrugated cardboard glued in position over some crumpled-up newspaper stuck to the backing sheet to make it three dimensional. Boxes are used to make the driver's cab; cheese cartons and thread spools are used for the wheels and cotton for the smoke. The tree is made from scraps of fabric, and the ground is represented by sand scattered or pressed onto wet glue. The center of the sun is made by sticking seeds or beans onto the paper, and its rays are cut from fabric.

FABRIC COLLAGE

Organization

A wide selection of patterned, plain, and textured fabric scraps should be collected and stored for general use in a large cardboard box in the classroom. Rummage sales are a useful source of cheap, interesting fabrics.

Materials

Fabric pieces and scraps; glue and brush; scissors; backing paper or cardboard, such as the side of a large cardboard box.

Technique

The shapes of the design are cut from the fabric pieces and arranged in position on the backing sheet. When the design is complete, the pieces are glued and pressed down firmly.

A decorative border of strips of material, ribbon, or braid can be added to the picture for extra effect.

Suitable themes for this type of collage design are birds of paradise, peacocks, harlequins, historical figures, circus animals and people, costumes of the world, and fantastic imaginary creatures.

TWO CHRISTMAS PICTURES

Organization

A collection of old Christmas cards can inspire designs for models, puppets, and friezes. For specific occasions such as Christmas, a collection of large-scale friezes around the classroom can be particularly effective. The whole class could be involved in this activity, with each group working on one aspect of the theme. The children should carefully plan and design their friezes before they begin to put them together.

Materials

A large sheet of fairly stiff paper; scissors; tissue paper; scraps of colored papers; black paper; scraps of colored ribbon, braid or foil; paints and brush; sponge; glue and brush.

Technique

To make the background for both pictures, dip a sponge in thin paint and dab

FIGURE 5-10
Fabric collage

it all over the sheet of paper on which the design is to be mounted, redipping the sponge with paint when necessary. For the church and building frieze, a blue or grey background might be most effective.

Balloon frieze   Cut out large balloon shapes from tissue or fancy colored paper and glue them onto the background paper as shown in Figure 5-11. Cut out shapes from the colored papers and glue them onto the balloons for decoration. Glue narrow strips of foil, paper, or fancy braid onto the background from the top edge of the frieze down to meet the balloons, to create the impression that the balloons are hanging. Cut out a paper or foil border and glue it onto the frieze to frame the picture.

Church and buildings frieze   Cut out a selection of church and building shapes from dark paper (white paper can be painted with dark-colored paint if no dark paper is available). Arrange the shapes side by side on the background paper, and when satisfied with the arrangement, glue the shapes in position. Draw a star on silver or gold paper, cut it out, and glue it onto the frieze above one of the buildings.

Further details can be added to the design, such as a host of angels cut from cardboard and decorated with colored scraps of paper and material.

Bells can be stenciled onto the frieze by using a piece of strong cardboard from which a bell shape has been cut as described in Chapter 8. Take care not to smudge the paint when using the stencil.

Frame the picture as described above.

FIGURE 5-11
Balloon frieze

FIGURE 5-12
Church-and-buildings frieze

Junk Models

The ideas given in this section are intended only as suggestions for ways in which junk materials can be used. At first the instructions can be followed quite rigidly, but after some practice, as the children gain confidence, these instructions should be used only as a guide. The children should always be encouraged to be inventive and imaginative, constantly adapting their ideas according to the materials available and the way a project develops.

A collection of junk will provide a wide range of useful materials for art and craft work. It is cheap, often free, readily available, and easily stored, all of which are important considerations for the teacher when he or she is planning work and the organization of the classroom.

ORGANIZING JUNK BOXES

It is essential to organize the junk if it is to be used successfully. It should never be stored in one large box as then the children will be unable to find small items when they are required. Items of junk should be sorted and stored in separate containers, such as shoe boxes or large plastic ice-cream cartons, and clearly labeled to show what they contain. They should be stored on shelves or in a cupboard in one area of the classroom within easy access of where the craft activities take place. Some items can be put in the same box, for example, tissue-paper scraps with pretty candy wrappers, buttons with beads, string with wool, and cotton with scraps of fur. Other boxes should contain items such as thread reels, corks, foam rubber, metal bottle caps, pipe cleaners, dried seeds and beans, feathers and straws, and anything else that might have a use in art and craft work. Several large, clearly labeled cardboard boxes can be stored nearby containing larger things, such as egg and cereal cartons, dishwashing liquid containers, and plastic bowls. Another large box should be reserved for material and fabric scraps. Large pieces of strong cardboard are often required for craft work and these can be provided by cutting out the sides and bases from cardboard boxes. These are easily obtained free of charge from shops and supermarkets. Cut the cardboard with scissors or a sharp knife and stack the sheets in a cardboard box. A pile of newspapers and magazines is also essential for the junk-box collection. It is important that the children are trained to use the junk boxes properly and to return leftover items to the correct boxes when their

work is finished. This is an excellent activity for sorting and reading practice. As the children get into the habit of bringing useful junk items into school, a good collection will soon be accumulated.

Finally, always make it clear to the children that they are responsible for clearing up the mess they make. This should be regarded as an important part of their work and their education. If the teacher always insists on this, in time the children will learn to create a minimum of mess while they are working. However, a certain amount of mess is inevitable with creative work.

BOATS

Organization

Craft work can often be integrated with other subjects in the curriculum. Making boats should include an introductory discussion about which materials will float, which will sink, and why. Children love exciting stories of long sea voyages, piracy, and the discovery of new lands.

Materials

Polystyrene boat Polystyrene tray; cork; cocktail stick; white plastic bag; scissors; waterproof glue and brush.

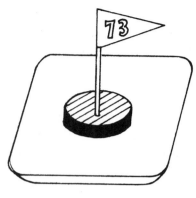

FIGURE 6-1
Polystyrene boat

Catamaran Two plastic dishwashing liquid containers; two strips of wood, such as two old rulers; two sticks; white plastic bag; scissors; waterproof glue and brush.

Power boat Balsa wood; sharp knife; two nails; hammer; strong rubber band; small piece of thin wood; strong adhesive tape; scissors.

Technique

Polystyrene boat Use a waterproof glue to attach a small section of cork which will hold the mast to a polystyrene tray. Cut a sail from a white plastic bag and glue it to one end of a cocktail stick. Push the other end of the cocktail stick into the cork, and the boat is complete.

Catamaran Attach the two strips of wood or rulers to the top of the plastic containers with a waterproof glue as shown in Figure 6-2. Make a hole in the top of each container with scissors. Take two sticks (the type used by gardeners for staking cuttings) and attach white plastic sails to the top of them with waterproof glue. Push the other end of the sticks as far as they will go into the holes made in the plastic containers. Glue all around the area where the sticks touch the plastic to hold the masts securely in place.

Power boat Using a sharp knife, cut the boat shape shown by the shaded area in Figure 6-3 from balsa wood.

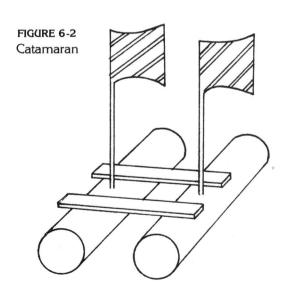

FIGURE 6-2
Catamaran

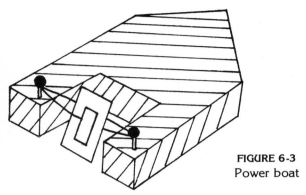

FIGURE 6-3
Power boat

them when all the material has been sold. Store them propped up in a corner of the classroom or in a cardboard box.

Materials

Windmill Tall cardboard box; a cardboard tube long enough to pass right through the cardboard box and protrude on both sides; the side of another cardboard box; scissors or sharp knife; paints and brush; glue and brush.

Castle Cardboard box; four dishwashing liquid containers; colored paper for the flags; four short sticks; glue and brush; paints and brush.

Technique

Windmill Cut the sails for the windmill out of one piece of cardboard cut from the side of a cardboard box and make a hole in the middle for the cardboard tube to pass through.

Stand the tall cardboard box on its end, and near to the top, make holes on opposite sides for the cardboard tube. Push the tube right through the box and the hole at the center of the sail so that a small section of the tube protrudes in front of the sails. A longer section of the cardboard tube should protrude at the back of the box.

Hammer two small nails on each side at the back of the boat as shown. Take a small rectangle of thin wood and put it in the middle of a strong rubber band. Secure the rubber on each side of the wood with a strip of strong tape. Loop the ends of the rubber band over the nails at the back of the boat.

When the piece of wood is turned and released it will act as a paddle, and the boat will be propelled across the surface of the water.

MODELS FROM LARGE BOXES

Organization

Long cardboard tubes can be obtained from shops that sell material. The tubes are at the center of the material rolls, and the shop is often pleased to dispose of

Apply glue to the area where the tube meets the sails at the front of the windmill. Decorate the windmill and sails with paints. The sails are moved by turning the cardboard tube at the back of the box or from inside if the box is large enough to allow a small child to crouch inside it. The children could take the windmill outside to see if they can adjust the sails so that the wind will drive them.

Castle Glue four plastic dishwashing-liquid containers to the top corners of an upturned cardboard box. Attach a brightly colored paper flag to each of four short sticks glued inside the tops of the containers. Cut egg-carton sections into strips and glue them around the edges of the box at the top as shown in Figure 6-5 to make the castle battlements. Paint the castle an appropriate color.

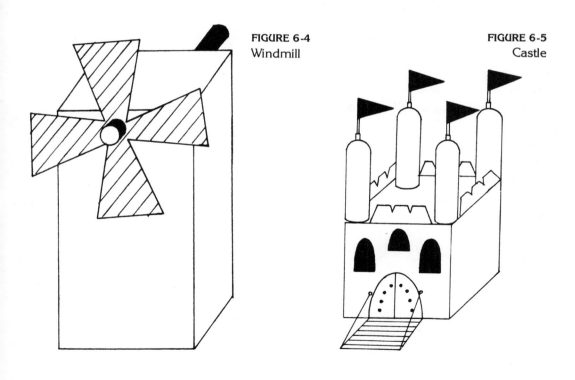

FIGURE 6-4
Windmill

FIGURE 6-5
Castle

TOTEM POLE
AND TRUCK

Organization

When making large-scale models it is often easier for the children to work on the floor in an area of the classroom reserved for this purpose. Cover the floor with newspaper before the project is started. When building a large model, allow the glue to dry between each stage so that the model will be as strong as possible.

Materials

Totem pole Selection of cardboard boxes; strong glue and glue brush; cardboard; paints and brush; scissors.

Truck Two large boxes; one smaller box; thick cardboard such as the side of a cardboard box; four paper fasteners; two paper plates; glue and brush; scissors; paints and brush.

Technique

Totem pole Build up the totem pole by gluing a variety of different shaped boxes on top of one another, allowing the glue

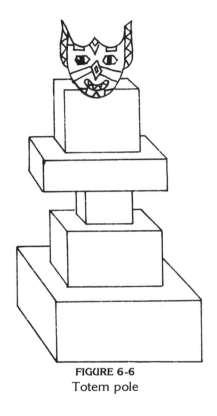

FIGURE 6-6
Totem pole

to dry before the next box is added. Use cardboard to make a picture of an animal's head or the head of an Indian chief and glue it to the top of the totem pole. Decorate the whole model with brightly colored paints and allow it to dry. A totem pole of this kind makes an interesting focal point around which to improvise a play.

Truck Close a cardboard box and secure the flaps with glue. Stand the box on its end. This forms the cab of the truck. Use scissors or a sharp knife to cut out a small window on each side. Cut away the opening flaps on the other large box and glue it to the back of the cab, with the cut-away side uppermost, as shown in Figure 6-7. Attach the smaller box to the front of the cab to make the engine, gluing down its opening flaps if necessary. Cut four large circles from the sides of spare cardboard boxes to make the truck's wheels and fasten these to the truck with paper fasteners. The wheels will revolve when the truck is moved. Glue two paper plates onto the front of the truck's cab as headlights. Paint the lights bright yellow and decorate the rest of the truck with paints.

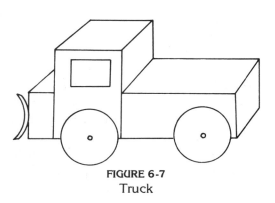

FIGURE 6-7
Truck

PAPIER-MÂCHÉ BALLOON SHAPES—PIG AND HUMPTY DUMPTY

Organization

The children can construct these papier-mâché shapes working in pairs, one child holding the slippery pasted balloon while the other continues building up the layers of papier-mâché. Be sure to cover the balloon with sufficient layers of paper and paste; about four layers are adequate.

Materials

Balloon; cooking oil; newspaper; paste; five corks or sections cut from a toilet paper roll; cardboard; pipe cleaners; glue and brush; scissors; paints and brush.

Technique

Cover the blown-up balloon with oil and then strips of newspaper dipped in paste (use the papier-mâché technique described in Chapter 2). Allow the papier-mâché to dry and then break the balloon. Decorate this papier-mâché shape to make an animal or character such as a pig or Humpty Dumpty.

FIGURE 6-8
Pig

color for his trousers on the lower half. When the pink paint has dried, paint on his features, hands, and arms.

FIGURE 6-9
Humpty Dumpty

Pig For the pig's legs, glue four corks onto the papier-mâché shape. Alternatively, cut a toilet paper roll into sections and use these. Glue another cork or toilet-paper-roll section onto the pig's face for a nose, or use a section cut from an egg carton. A twisted pipe cleaner or a curled strip of paper can be glued to the end of the body for a tail. The pig's ears can be made by cutting out two triangles from cardboard and attaching them to the head by a small flap folded back at the base of each ear. Bend the points of the ears down toward the pig's nose. Paint the pig in any colors you like.

Humpty Dumpty Humpty Dumpty has two sections cut from a toilet-paper roll for his feet and two ears cut from cardboard or pink foam rubber and glued onto the side of his face. He is then covered with a layer of thick pink paint on the top half of his body and a bright

EASTER-CHICKS PICTURE

Organization

One group of children can work on the background for this picture while another group makes the papier-mâché balloon shapes for the chicks. The chicks should be mounted on a sheet of strong paper or cardboard which has been decorated by using any collage or printing technique. One suitable technique is to cover the background with cut or torn tissue-paper shapes pasted onto the paper.

Materials

Balloon; cooking oil; newspaper; yellow tissue paper; paste and brush; red or orange felt scraps; cardboard; scissors; glue and brush; colored gummed paper; a sheet of paper or cardboard on which to mount the balloon shapes.

Technique

Cover the balloon with oil and then strips of newspaper dipped in paste, as described in Chapter 2. Allow the papier-mâché to dry, break the balloon, and use a sharp knife or scissors to cut it in half lengthways. Cover the rounded surfaces of the half balloons with several layers of yellow tissue paper and paste, so that the newspaper cannot be seen. Allow the tissue paper to dry. Carefully glue all around the rims and attach the papier-mâché shapes to the decorated backing paper in the positions required. Add details to make the yellow balloon shapes into Easter chicks, using scraps from the material and junk boxes. Cut legs from cardboard and cover them with orange gummed paper cut to shape. Cardboard wings can be glued to the sides of the chicks' bodies and bent outwards to increase the three-dimensional effect of the picture. Orange or red felt scraps can be used to make beaks. Cut out diamond-shaped pieces, fold them in half, and glue them to the chicks' faces by the fold. Add eyes to the chicks' faces by using paint, buttons, or circles cut from gummed paper.

FLYING BALLOONS

FIGURE 6-10
Easter-chicks picture

Organization

Objects displayed hanging from the ceiling add an extra dimension to the classroom and do not take up valuable shelf or wall space. Flying balloons make an exciting classroom display and they can be linked to science, history, and geography projects. They can provoke discussions about the sort of music their flight suggests or they can be used to inspire exciting adventure stories.

Materials

Balloon; cooking oil; strips of newspaper; paste; string; small box; paints and brush; glue and brush; Plasticine.

Technique

Cover the blown-up balloon with oil and then strips of newspaper dipped in paste as described in Chapter 2. Allow the papier-mâché to dry and then break the balloon, leaving the balloon shape intact. Decorate the balloon as colorfully as possible, using paints or material from the junk box. Hanging below the balloon is a small box painted to resemble a wicker basket. Cut off two lengths of string long enough to pass over the top of the balloon and hang below it to support the basket underneath. Tie the two strings together in the middle so that four strings hang down from the knot as shown in Figure 6-11. Glue the knot to the top of the balloon and tie the strings to small holes made in each side of the basket. Adjust the length of the strings to make the basket level.

Make small model people in Plasticine to stand inside the basket. Suspend the balloon from the ceiling by a short length of string fastened at one end to the balloon with tape and at the other end to a thumbtack stuck in the ceiling. Hang

FIGURE 6-11
Flying balloon

the balloon in a draft so that it will sway in the breeze.

PAPIER-MÂCHÉ BOWLS

Organization

The whole class could try making different things with papier-mâché balloon shapes in the same lesson. There are many possibilities, some of which are described in Chapter 2 and in the previous sections of this chapter. The end result will be an interesting variety of masks, models, and bowls.

When the shapes are made into bowls, encourage the children to look at patterns on pots, bowls, and dishes to get ideas for decorating them. The pottery, both ancient and modern, of Mexico and Peru can be particularly inspiring.

Materials

Balloon; cooking oil; newspaper; paste; scissors; paints and brush; varnish or lacquer.

Technique

Cover a blown-up balloon with oil, then strips of newspaper and paste as de-

scribed in Chapter 2. When the papier-mâché shape is completely dry, pop the balloon and cut the papier-mâché shape in half to make two bowls. Use sharp scissors to trim the rims of the bowls to make a neat edge.

Paint the inside and outside of the bowls. When the paint is dry, apply a layer of varnish or lacquer all over the painted surfaces of the bowls.

THINGS TO WEAR: HEADDRESS AND BINOCULARS

Organization

Dressing-up clothes can be made for a specific occasion or added to a general collection in a dressing-up box. If there is a collection of dressing-up clothes in the classroom, spontaneous improvisation in drama and dance is always possible.

Materials

Headdress Corrugated cardboard; feathers; scissors; glue and brush; paper clip.

Binoculars Two toilet paper rolls; silver foil; string; scissors; glue and brush.

FIGURE 6-12
Looking into a decorated
papier-mâché bowl

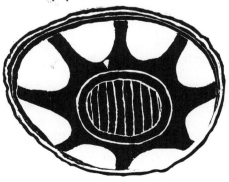

Technique

Headdress Cut out a band of corrugated cardboard about two inches (five centimeters) wide and long enough to pass right around the head. Dip the quill ends of some feathers in glue and push them into the holes of the corrugated cardboard at intervals. Wind the band of corrugated cardboard around the forehead, and after adjusting it to fit, fasten the two ends of the cardboard together with a paper clip. It may be easier if one child helps another with this task. Remove the headdress and apply glue to the join to make it more secure. Paint the band and feathers if desired.

Binoculars Cut out two strips of aluminum foil slightly wider than the length of a toilet paper roll and long enough to pass right around it with a slight overlap. Apply glue to the toilet paper roll and wrap the foil around it. Glue the section where the foil overlaps to ensure a neat join. Fold the ends of the foil to the inside of the tube. Repeat this procedure with the second toilet paper roll; then glue them both together, side by side. Make small holes at one end on each side of the binoculars and tie a length of string through them so that the binoculars can be hung around the neck.

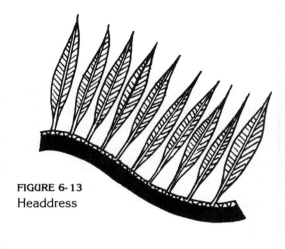

FIGURE 6-13
Headaddress

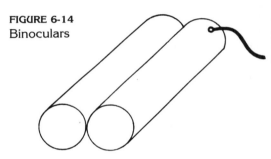

FIGURE 6-14
Binoculars

SOLDIER'S OUTFIT

Organization

This craft work can easily be linked to a history project. The children will enjoy dressing up in costumes they have made themselves and acting out historical events will help them to remember the stories they have heard.

Materials

Helmet Thin cardboard; scissors; paste and brush; glue and brush or stapler; paints and brush.

Sword Cardboard from the side of a large cardboard box; glue and brush or stapler; paints and brush.

Shield Thin cardboard; scissors; glue and brush or stapler; paints and brush; washed yogurt-carton tops.

Technique

Helmet Take a rectangular sheet of thin cardboard and draw a tall M shape at the center of one of the long sides of the cardboard as shown in Figure 6-15. The width of the M should be approximately the same width as the face of the child who is to wear the helmet. Cut the M shape out and paint the rest of the cardboard in a suitable color for the helmet. When the paint is dry, roll the cardboard into a cylinder which fits over the child's head and rests on the shoulders. Glue or staple the two ends of the cardboard together at the back of the helmet.

Sword The sword needs to be strong, so it is made from cardboard cut from the side of a large cardboard box. Cut out the pieces for the handle and the blade and glue them together. Alternatively, cut out the whole shape from one piece of cardboard if the side of the box is large enough. Decorate the handle with paints, and paint the blade of the sword gray or gold to resemble metal.

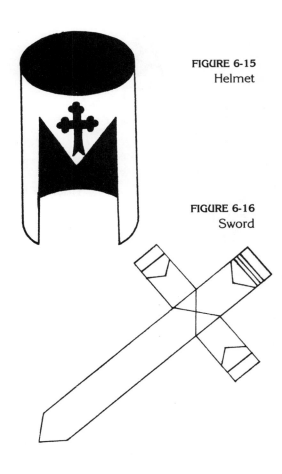

FIGURE 6-15
Helmet

FIGURE 6-16
Sword

Shield   Cut out a shield shape from the side of a cardboard box. Paint a horizontal and a vertical black line on the shield to divide it into sections as shown in Figure 6-17. Glue clean yogurt-carton tops onto two or more of the sections. Hold the shield with a strip of cardboard glued at both ends to the back of the shield to make a loop.

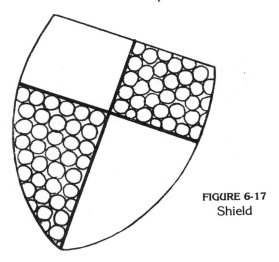

FIGURE 6-17
Shield

cess's hat make attractive hats for Christmas or for characters to wear in plays. The floral hat can make a pretty Easter bonnet or a hat to wear to a birthday party. A stapler is very useful for making hats. When the correct circumference has been measured around the head, the cardboard can be quickly secured in position with a staple.

Materials

Crown   Cardboard; scissors; silver foil; colored gummed paper; fur scraps; candy papers; yogurt-carton tops; glue and brush; stapler.

Princess's hat   Large piece of thin cardboard; ruler and pencil; scissors; glue and brush; stapler; silver foil; crepe paper; yogurt-carton tops; decorative paper; paints and brush.

Floral Hat   Plate; crepe paper; material; tissue paper; scissors; glue and brush.

HATS

Organization

Basic hat designs can be adapted for different occasions by decorating them in a suitable way. The crown and prin-

Technique

Crown   Take a rectangular sheet of cardboard and cut a row of triangular shapes along one of its long sides to make the top of the crown. Draw circles on the cut-away pieces of cardboard and

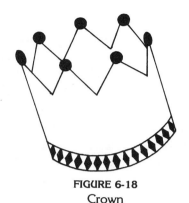

FIGURE 6-18
Crown

cut these out. Glue them onto the points of the crown. Decorate the crown by gluing on shapes cut from silver foil, colored papers, fur scraps, yogurt-carton tops, and pretty candy wrappers. Use a strip of silver foil to make a border along the lower rim of the crown, laying it on the card so that it overlaps the rim. Fold back the overlapping silver foil to make a neat edge before gluing it in position. Roll the card into a cylinder to fit the child's head and secure the ends at the back with glue or staples.

Princess's hat Draw the shape shown in Figure 6-19, using a ruler for the straight lines. Strip *a* must be long enough to pass around the child's head and overlap at the ends.

Strip *c* is drawn about a quarter of the way along strip *a*. Strips *a*, *b*, and *c*

should all be of the same length and approximately one and one-quarter inch (approximately three centimeters) wide. Cut out the shape and bend strip *a* to encircle the child's head. Overlap the ends slightly and glue or staple them in position. Bend strip *b* over to meet strip *a* and glue or staple the end inside the band. Now fold strip *c* over the top and at right angles to strip *b* and fasten *c* to band *a* in the same way.

Make a small cone from spare cardboard and glue the base to the top of the hat. Cut out strips of silver foil, crepe paper, or both and glue the strips together at one end. Glue the bunch of streamers to the top of the princess's hat and decorate the rest of the hat with paints, yogurt-carton tops, and fancy papers.

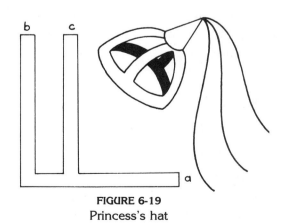

FIGURE 6-19
Princess's hat

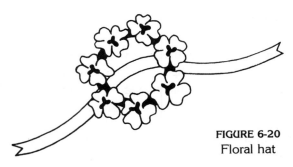

FIGURE 6-20
Floral hat

sections of different lengths, a family group could be made. The widths of the cardboard tubes can also be graded to make a series of people from thin to fat.

Sections cut from cardboard rolls can also be used to make scenery for a puppet theater or as a background for these model people. For example, the tubes could represent tree trunks with dyed or painted cotton attached to their tops for foliage.

Floral hat Cut out a long strip of crepe paper or fancy material and glue the middle of it to the back of a paper plate so that two ties hang down on each side as shown in Figure 6-20. Make flowers from tissue paper and glue these all around the rim of the plate. Flowers can be made by cutting out lots of petals, bunching them together, and gluing or stapling them at one end. Alternatively, the children may have their own methods for making paper flowers, or they may invent their own methods if given the chance.

Materials

Tube model Cardboard tube (a toilet-paper roll is rather small but could be used); material scraps; ribbon or braid; cardboard; egg-carton section; button; scissors; paints and brush; glue and brush.

Paper-bag model Paper bag; newspaper; string; two yogurt cartons; cardboard; wool or tissue; paper scraps; scissors; glue and brush; paints and brush.

MODEL PEOPLE

Organization

The model of the woman is made from a section of a long roll around which material is wound. By using a number of

Technique

Tube model Paint half of the cardboard tube with pink paint. Cut out a strip of material long enough to wrap loosely around the cardboard tube and wide enough to cover half of its length, with

FIGURE 6-21
Tube model

Decorate the hat with paint and a pretty button glued in place to resemble a flower. Paint facial features and allow them to dry before using the model.

Paper-bag model Stuff the end of a paper bag with a ball of newspaper to make the head and tie below it with string. Stuff more newspaper into the bag and glue the open end of the bag around the bases of the two upturned yogurt cartons as shown in Figure 6-22. Cut two arms and hands from cardboard and glue these onto the sides of the model. Glue cotton balls or tightly rolled scraps of tissue paper onto the head for hair. Finally, paint the model and allow it to dry.

some allowance for a hem. Make a hem at the lower edge of the skirt and sew or glue it in place. Apply a band of glue all around the model's waist and attach the top of the skirt to it, making pleats where necessary. Glue a strip of ribbon or braid around the model's waist to cover the raw edge of the material. Cut two arms and hands from cardboard and glue them to the sides of the tube.

Cut two feet from the cardboard allowing a flap of cardboard at the end with which to attach the feet to the base of the cardboard tube with glue. Glue a section of an egg carton or a small upturned pot to the top of the model for a hat.

FIGURE 6-22
Paper-bag model

CONE AND WIRE FIGURES

Organization

This technique can be used to make the basic forms for a wide variety of characters. These could include a Christmas fairy or angel, characters from nursery rhymes and stories, or people from other lands.

Materials

Cardboard; pencil; scissors; dinner plate or other round object to help with drawing a circle; gardening stick; wire; Ping-Pong ball; a box of tissues; paste; material scraps; wool scraps; glue and brush; paints and brush.

Technique

Use a dinner plate, round dishpan, or similar sized object to draw a circle on cardboard. Cut out the circle and cut a line along a radius. Push the stick through the center of the circle and bend the cardboard around to make a cone. Use glue or staples to secure the cone as shown in Figure 6-23. Twist some wire around the stick about half way between the top of the cone skirt and the top of the stick. Bend the wire into arm

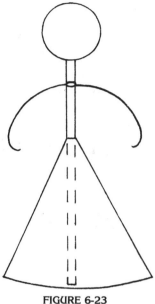

FIGURE 6-23
Cone and wire figure

shapes. Make a hole in a Ping-Pong ball and push the ball onto the top of the stick. Use tissues dipped in paste to build up layers of papier-mâché on the arms and body of the model until a satisfactory shape is made.

When the papier-mâché is thoroughly dry, use paints and material scraps to decorate the skirt, body, and arms of the model to create the character required. Paint on the facial features and glue scraps of wool on top of the Ping-Pong ball for hair. Further details can be added, such as a handbag, glasses, or a walking stick.

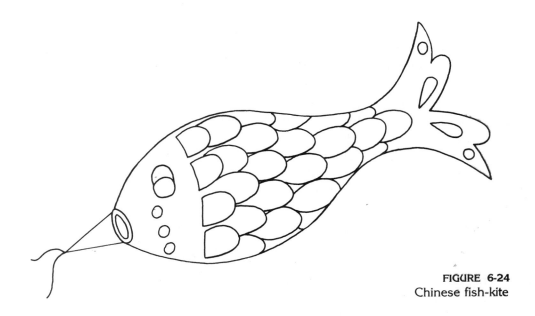

FIGURE 6-24
Chinese fish-kite

CHINESE FISH-KITE

Organization

The results of this activity make a striking display in a classroom when suspended from the ceiling. However, the models are very fragile and unlikely to fly well so it is not recommended that they be used as kites.

Materials

Tissue paper; pencil; scissors; wire; wire cutters; string; glue and brush.

Technique

Place two sheets of tissue paper on top of each other on a flat work surface and carefully draw the outline of a large fish on the upper sheet of paper, using as much of the tissue paper as possible. Cut out the shape of the fish through both layers of tissue. Glue the two fish shapes together around the outer edges, leaving the mouth open. Bend the wire into a circle to fit the hole made by the fish's mouth and secure the ends of the wire circle by twisting them around each other. Cut off any surplus wire with the wire cutters. Tie two pieces of string opposite each other on the wire circle and tie the strings together at a point about 12 inches (thirty centimeters) from the wire. This string loop will be used to suspend the finished model from the ceiling. Insert the wire circle very carefully into the fish's mouth, folding over the edges of the tissue-paper mouth to enclose the wire and gluing the tissue in position there.

Decorate the fish's body with tissue-paper scales or lightweight scraps from the junk boxes.

The fish can be suspended from the ceiling by the string tied to its mouth. To hang the fish horizontally, attach another string to its body, near to the tail.

SIMPLE ANIMALS

Organization

These creatures are suitable for very young children to make. They could be linked together by a common theme or project such as "The Animal Kingdom" or "Creatures, Great and Small."

Materials

Pig One large and one small potato; five cocktail sticks; pipe cleaner.

Caterpillar Cardboard egg carton; scissors; two buttons; cardboard; paints and brush; glue and brush.

Spider Cardboard egg carton; paints and brush; scissors; pipe cleaners; string.

Hedgehog Plasticine; straws.

Technique

Pig Push a cocktail stick into one end of the large potato and spear the small potato on the end. Push in four cocktail sticks for legs and a pipe cleaner for a tail. Wind the pipe-cleaner tail around a pencil to make it curly.

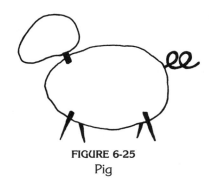

FIGURE 6-25
Pig

Caterpillar Cut a cardboard egg carton in half to make two strips with three sections in each. Decorate one section to make a caterpillar by painting the egg-

FIGURE 6-26
Caterpillar

carton section green, and when dry, painting patterns on its body. Glue two buttons in position for its eyes and two small strips cut from cardboard on top of his head to make its feelers.

Spider Cut out one section of the cardboard egg carton and paint it in any color suitable for a spider. When dry, use scissors to make eight holes around the lower edge, as shown in Figure 6-27, and one hole in the top. To make the legs, cut four pipe cleaners in half and push them through the holes, bending

FIGURE 6-27
Spider

the ends over to secure them to the body. Thread a length of string through the hole in the top of the egg-carton section and tie a knot underneath inside the body so that the spider can be suspended from a ceiling, doorway, window frame, or corner of the room.

Hedgehog Mold the hedgehog's body shape in Plasticine. Cut straws into quarters and press these into the Plasticine to make the spikes.

FIGURE 6-28
Hedgehog

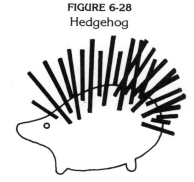

LARGE-SCALE MONSTER

Organization

The monster may require several work sessions spread over a few days before it is finished, so reserve an area of the classroom where it can be safely left without causing too much disturbance to the organization of the rest of the room.

Materials

Several large cardboard boxes of assorted shapes and sizes; glue and brush; four tin cans; cardboard egg cartons; a long strip of material; scissors; paints and brush.

Technique

Place several boxes side by side on the floor to make the monster's body. Put two smaller boxes at one end to make a head and nose, as shown in Figure 6-29. Glue all the boxes together. When the glue is dry, turn the monster upside down and glue four or more tin cans to the base for its legs. Allow the glue to set hard, then turn the monster the right way up. Glue cardboard egg-carton sections all over the body. To make the tail cut out a long strip of material the same width as the egg cartons and glue egg-carton sections along it. Attach one end of the material to the end of the monster's body. Cut out two large circles for eyes from the side of a spare cardboard box and glue them onto the sides of the monster's face.

When all the glue is completely dry, cover the monster with thick paint. Colors like green and brown will suggest a real creature such as a crocodile, but imaginary monsters and dragons can be created by using a more exciting range of colors. When the base coat of paint is dry, paint patterns on the creature's body, head, and tail.

HANGING BIRD AND CAT

Organization

To make a mobile, several of these creatures can be hung from a wire coat hanger that has been bent to any suitable

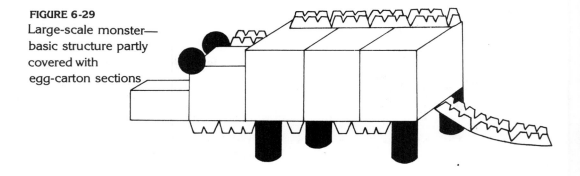

FIGURE 6-29
Large-scale monster—
basic structure partly
covered with
egg-carton sections

shape. They can also be hung individually from window frames or near open windows so that they move in the breeze. Another way of displaying them is to hang them from the stripped frame of an old or broken umbrella opened and suspended by its handle from the ceiling.

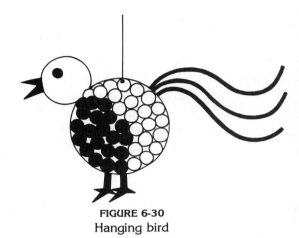

FIGURE 6-30
Hanging bird

Materials

Bird Cardboard; pencil; scissors; silver foil; colored gummed paper; glue and brush; clean yogurt-carton tops; string.

Cat Cardboard; pencil; scissors; string; two buttons; pipe cleaners or white paper; glue and brush; paints and brush or crayons.

Technique

Bird Draw one large and one small circle next to each other on a piece of cardboard to form the head and body of the bird as shown in Figure 6-30. Cut out the shape drawn on the cardboard with scissors. Cut strips of foil about 12 inches (thirty centimeters) long and three-quarters of an inch (two centimeters) wide and glue these onto the back of the bird's body for his tail. Cover its head and legs with brown gummed paper. Its beak and feet could be covered

with yellow or orange gummed paper. Make an eye from a leftover scrap of colored paper and stick it onto the bird's face. Cover the bird's body with yogurt-carton tops glued onto the card. Circles of red gummed paper can be glued to the bird's breast to turn it into a robin. Suspend the bird from a length of string tied to a small hole on the bird's back.

Cat Draw the shape of the cat's head and body on a sheet of cardboard and cut it out. Cut out two large eye shapes from his face. Make two small holes through the cardboard just above the eyes and use these to suspend a button in each cut-away space from a short length of string. Glue pipe cleaners, strips of white paper, or long bristles cut from a broom onto the cat's face for whiskers. Make the cat's tail from a circle of cardboard or paper. Draw a spiral pattern on it as shown in Figure 6-31. Cut along the line and glue the center of the spiral to the back of the cat's body for the tail. Decorate the cat with paints or crayons.

Tie a length of string to a small hole made in the top of the cat's head and use this to suspend the cat from the ceiling.

A leaping frog with two spirals for its legs can be made in a similar way.

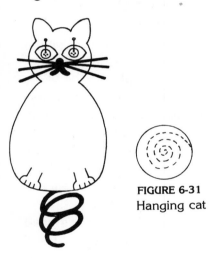

FIGURE 6-31
Hanging cat

FISH MOBILE

Organization

This mobile is an ideal way to use up any odd pieces of cane left over from making baskets. The cane needs to be soaked in water for a few minutes to make it sufficiently pliable for bending into fish shapes.

Materials

Cane; thread; buttons; scissors; glue and brush; wire; wire cutters.

Technique

Bend pieces of cane to make the fish shapes shown in Figure 6-32, tying thread around the place where the cane overlaps near to the tail. Suspend buttons from short lengths of thread to make the fish's eye. Cut a length of wire to make the top support for the mobile and shorter lengths of wire for the lower supports.

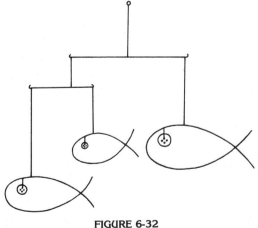

FIGURE 6-32
Fish mobile

Suspend the fishes and the supports from pieces of thread as shown in the illustration. Adjust the position of each piece of thread until all the fishes and the wire supports are horizontal. If necessary, secure the thread with a blob of glue where it is tied to the cane or wire. Suspend the mobile from the ceiling by a short length of string or thread.

FISH TANK

Organization

This activity can be adapted to the number of children who wish to participate in it. One child alone can make a fairly small-scale underwater scene, or a whole group working together can use a very large cardboard box to make a bigger, more adventurous model.

Materials

Cardboard box; scissors; cardboard; scraps of material and felt; fancy papers, such as candy wrappers; silver foil; glue and brush; blue and green tissue paper; paste and brush; paints and brush; thread.

Technique

Close the flaps of a cardboard box and secure them in place with glue. Turn the box over and use this as the base of the model. Use scissors or a sharp knife to cut away most of the front of the box. Leave a straight border at the sides. To give the impression of waves, cut a wavy border along the top and bottom of the front of the box as shown in Figure 6-33. Paste torn pieces of green and blue tissue paper over the sides and floor of the inside of the box. Overlapping the tissue will make the tones of color more interesting. This creates an underwater effect inside the tank. Another way to do this is with the graining and stippling technique described in Chapter 4, using tones of green and blue. Paint the outside of the box. Cut fish shapes from the cardboard and decorate them with scraps of material, felt, tissue, and fancy papers glued onto their bodies. Make them as colorful and attractive as possible. Pierce small

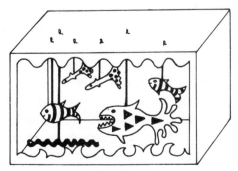

FIGURE 6-33
Fish tank

holes in the upper parts of the fish shapes and tie pieces of thread to the fish through these holes. Make several holes in the top of the box with scissors. Suspend the fish from the top of the cardboard box by threading the free end of the thread up through the holes in the top of the box and securing them there with a blob of glue.

The back of the tank can also be cut away and replaced by a sheet of tissue paper so that the light will shine through when the model is displayed in front of a window.

LARGE-SCALE WIRE-AND-PAPIER-MÂCHÉ ELEPHANT

Organization

Chicken wire is a type of flexible wire netting and can be bought in hardware stores.

It is a good idea to plan as accurately as possible the sizes of the pieces of chicken wire required to make the elephant's body, head, and limbs before going to buy it. Suppliers may be prepared to cut the wire into the correct sizes for each section at no extra charge.

Materials

Chicken wire; wire cutters; thin wire; newspaper; large quantity of paste in a bucket or dishpan; paints and brush.

Technique

The basic shape of the elephant is made from pieces of chicken wire cut to size and molded into shape. The elephant's body is made in sections that are joined together with pieces of wire.

One piece of chicken wire is required to make a large cylinder for its body, and four smaller cylinders of chicken wire are needed for its legs. A triangular-shaped sheet of chicken wire can be made into a long cone for its head and trunk. Two flat pieces of chicken wire are needed for its ears and an odd strip of wire for its tail. Two cones made from triangular pieces of wire are used for its tusks.

Cut out the chicken-wire shapes required for these sections. Bend the wire into the correct shapes for the body, head, and legs and secure the ends of the wire together. With chicken wire, this can be done by threading pieces of thin, flexible wire through the holes on both sides of the join and then twisting the ends together to secure them. Join the head and legs to the elephant's body in

FIGURE 6-34
Large-scale wire-and-papier-mâché elephant

this way. Use another piece of wire to attach the two ear flaps and the tusks to the elephant's head. Attach a long, thin cylinder of wire to its rear end for a tail. Be sure that the basic wire structure of the elephant is strong and stands well on its legs without rocking or falling over. If necessary, weave more strands of wire in and out of the chicken wire at the joins to hold them firmly in place.

The next stage is to cover the wire shape with strips of newspaper which have been dipped in paste. Weave some of the newspaper strips that make the first layer in and out of the chicken wire to hold them securely in position and to make a good base for subsequent layers. Do not get the newspaper too wet with paste or it will not stay in position on the wire. Build up about four or five layers of newspaper; then allow the papier-mâché to dry completely.

Paint the elephant all over. To get ideas for decorating the elephant, the children could look at pictures of Indian elephants in procession. For a professional finish, apply a layer of varnish all over the elephant when the paint is dry.

MODEL SCENE

Organization

This activity can be inspired by a visit, a vacation, or even a photograph. It can be a fairly modest project, representing a house or farm as shown in Figure 6-35, or it can be as ambitious as the children wish to make it, with rows of houses in streets with traffic lights, trees, and shops. A model of this type will give the children great opportunities for using techniques already learned, and it will stimulate them to invent all sorts of ways of making models and solving problems.

Materials

A piece of hard board or very strong cardboard cut from the side of a large box for the base; chicken wire; wire cutters; tape; newspaper; paste; scissors; paints and brush; cardboard boxes for the house shown below; cotton; glue and brush; cellophane; material scraps; small

FIGURE 6-35
Model scene

gravel chips; used matches (wooden ones are best); toilet paper roll; tissue paper; small twigs or pipe cleaners; small boxes for the vehicles; four paper fasteners; Plasticine or clay.

Technique

Cut a piece of chicken wire to a suitable size and shape to make the contours of a hill, as shown in Figure 6-35. Bend the wire into shape and place it on the board or cardboard base, in the position required for the hill. Secure it in place with tape. Cover the wire and the flat surface of the rest of the model with strips of newspaper soaked in paste. Continue in this way until four layers of newspaper have been built up; then allow this papier-mâché covering to dry. When dry, paint the hill and the base of the model to represent the ground.

While the painted base is drying, make a house from a suitably sized cardboard box. Make a roof for the house by cutting out a section of a cardboard box as shown in Figure 6-35. Glue a small box to the roof to represent a chimney and glue some cotton on top of it for smoke.

Cut out window shapes and cover them with pieces of cellophane glued to the inside of the box to resemble glass. Make curtains for each window from scraps of material and glue these in position inside the box. Paint any further details on the house, such as tiles for the roof, a number or name on the door, and the pattern of the bricks on the walls.

When the base of the model is completely dry, attach the house to it with glue and paint a path leading from the door of the house to the edge of the model. Fill in the path with small chips of gravel held in place with glue. Make fences and a gate from matchsticks to enclose the garden. Construct the fence in sections on a flat surface before attaching it to the model. The matchsticks are arranged in a simple pattern, such as the one shown in Figure 6-35, glued in position, and left to dry. When dry, each section can be attached to the model with glue.

The tree is made by painting a toilet paper roll a suitable color for the trunk. Crumple up some green or brown tissue paper into a loose ball and glue this on top of the toilet paper roll. Cut out leaf shapes from tissue paper and glue them onto the tissue-paper ball. Glue the tree to the base of the model. Make flowers for the garden by gluing small scraps of tissue paper, cut into petal shapes, onto the end of small twigs or sections of a pipe cleaner. Push the stem of each flower into a small ball of Plasticine and press this down onto the base.

A car or truck can be made from small

boxes by using the technique described previously in this chapter. It can be attached to the base of the model with glue or left to move freely.

The man, dog, and sheep can be molded from Plasticine or made from clay. The sheep are very effective if made from white or grey clay with black underglaze color dabbed on with a paintbrush to give them black faces. After the firing they should be dipped in transparent glaze and fired again. A black and white sheepdog can be made by using the same technique. Details of these processes are given in Chapter 10.

CHRISTMAS DECORATIONS: POLYHEDRON AND SPHERE

Organization

These models are built up in sections. Therefore it is possible for each child in a group to make one section of the final model. When the children have mastered the basic techniques, allow them to experiment with different materials to make models on different scales. Even yogurt-carton tops can be used to construct a tiny polyhedron.

At some stage in the activity introduce the word *polyhedron* (the name for a solid body bounded by many plane faces) to describe the shape of the first decoration.

Materials

Thin colored cardboard; scissors; glue and brush; staples; foil; colored paper and glitter for decoration.

Technique

Polyhedron   Cut out twenty circles from colored cardboard and draw an equilateral triangle in each, as shown in Figure 6-36. Fold the cardboard surrounding each triangle down to form three flaps, which are used to join the faces of the polyhedron together. Use these flaps to join five of the shapes together to make a shallow cone, as shown in Figure 6-37. Repeat this procedure with five more of the shapes. Now join ten of the shapes together to make a long strip, as shown in Figure 6-38. Join the ends together to make a ring. Attach one cone of shapes above the ring and one cone of shapes below the ring to make the shape shown in Figure 6-39.

Try using this technique with a variety of fairly stiff, fancy papers. The twenty cardboard circles with which the poly-

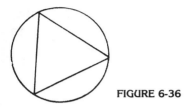

FIGURE 6-36

FIGURE 6-37

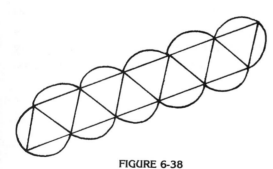

FIGURE 6-38

FIGURE 6-39

hedron is made can be decorated before construction with silver foil, candy wrappers, magazine pictures, or tissue paper pasted on. Children will also enjoy sprinkling glitter onto the decoration after applying glue to one or more of its faces.

Suspend the polyhedron from the ceiling by a piece of string.

Sphere of cones Draw circles on a piece of cardboard and cut them out. Cut a radius line to the center of each circle and bring one side of the cut cardboard over the other to form a cone. Glue or staple the sides together. Repeat this procedure until about twenty cones of approximately the same size have been made.

This step will provide enough cones with which to start the construction of the model. More cones can be made when required, as the model progresses. Join the cone shapes together to make a circle with the narrow ends of the cones pointing inward, toward the center, as shown in Figure 6-40.

Add more cones above and below this circle, securing them all in position with glue or staples, until a spherical shape has been made. The narrow ends of all the cones should point toward the center of the original circle, so the cone right on top, for example, should point vertically down.

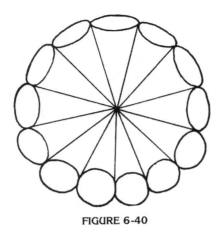

FIGURE 6-40

This is the basic form of the decoration. The original circles of cardboard can be decorated with colored and fancy papers before they are made into cones. Remember that it is the inside and *not* the outside of the cone that must be decorated; the outside will be hidden on the finished model.

Suspend the sphere from a piece of string or thread tied at one end to a small hole in the cardboard.

CHRISTMAS CHARACTERS

Organization

As Christmas is such a busy time for teachers and children alike, some quick and easy Christmas decorations are in-

valuable. These two Christmas characters are simple but can be decorated elaborately if time permits.

Materials

Angel Cardboard; paints and brush; material scraps; cotton or strips of yellow wool; glue and brush; stick.

Santa Claus Dishwashing liquid container; cardboard; scissors; glue and brush; red material; paints and brush; cotton.

Technique

Angel Draw the angel shape shown in Figure 6-41 on cardboard and cut it out. Decorate the angel with paint and pretty material scraps glued onto her dress.

FIGURE 6-41
Angel

Glue pieces of cotton or strips of yellow wool to her head for hair. Allow the paint and glue to dry and then bend the lower strips of cardboard around to the back to make a circle. Glue this in position and attach a stick to the inside of the cardboard circle at the back, so that the angel can be held and used as a puppet if required.

Santa Claus Cut out two arm and hand shapes from cardboard and glue one on each side of a dishwashing liquid container. Cover the hands, head, and neck with thick pink paint. The top of the dishwashing liquid container forms the

head and neck of the model. Cut out pieces of red material with which to cover the arms and the body of the figure below the painted area.

Cut out a large triangle of red material for Santa Claus's hat and sew the sides together to make a cone. Stitch or glue a narrow hem along the base of the hat. Turn the hat inside out to hide all the seams and attach it to the top of the plastic container with glue. Paint on the facial features and allow them to dry. Use cotton for the hat trim, eyebrows, moustache, beard, and sleeve and coat trim.

A WISE KING

Organization

This is a fairly large-scale model whose basic structure is very simple, but its decoration can be as sophisticated as the children wish to make it. It is therefore suitable for children of a wide range in age.

Materials

Cardboard; balloon; newspaper; paste; paints and brush; large piece of fancy material for the cloak; material scraps; wool scraps; scissors; glue and brush; cotton; small box; gold, silver, or any fancy papers.

FIGURE 6-42
Santa Claus

Technique

Cover a blown-up balloon with newspaper and paste (described in Chapter 2). Use a large sheet of cardboard to make a tall cone for the body (described in Chapter 6). Cut off the top (pointed end) of the cone and glue the balloon shape on top in its place. It is easier to apply the glue to the cone than to the balloon. Allow the glue to set hard; then paint the king's face pink. When dry, carefully paint features on the face and add lengths of wool or curled paper strips to the top of the head for his hair. Make a crown (described in Chapter 6) and glue it on top of the king's head. Make a triangular-shaped cloak from material to wrap around the king's cone body. Glue or stitch hems to hide the raw edges of the material. Glue the cloak around the king's neck. Attach cotton balls or a strip of braid around the neck on top of the cloak to cover the join. This also makes an attractive trim for the cloak.

Decorate any part of the cardboard cone body not covered by the cloak with fancy material scraps. Make hands from pink felt or foam rubber and glue them onto the cone. Alternatively, make hands from papier-mâché, paint them when dry, and glue them onto the cardboard

FIGURE 6-43
Wise king

cone. Cover a small box with silver, gold, or fancy paper and glue this to the hands of the model king so that he is carrying a gift.

Three kings can be made in this way, each decorated with different materials. The presents carried by the kings can vary in shape and size. Elaborately shaped containers can be molded in papier-mâché, allowed to dry, and then decorated with paints and varnish.

Further adornments can be added to the cloaks: sequins, braid, buttons, or embroidered motifs.

Greeting Cards

With the mass of commercially produced cards available in the stores, why make your own? The obvious answer to this question is a financial one. Cards are becoming increasingly expensive to buy, but a homemade card can cost next to nothing to make. Dozens of cards can be made for the price of a few bought ones. Also, the homemade card will be unique. The time and care taken to make the card will show the sincerity of the sender/maker and the message he or she wishes to convey.

To make a reasonably professional-looking card, certain basic equipment will be required. For the card shape itself, stiff paper or thin cardboard should be used. The shape of the card should be cut out with a pair of sharp scissors to ensure a neat, crisp edge. A ruler and a set square will be useful for drawing good straight lines and making accurate right-angled corners for the basic card shape and in the decoration as well, where required. A variety of tools for decoration should include pencils, paints, crayons, and felt-tip pens. A suitable adhesive will be needed for mounting decorations and for various other jobs in card making.

For a good effect, the card must have a crisp, clean fold at the center or where the fold is to be. This can be achieved by scoring the card. To do this, place a ruler on the card along the line where the fold is required. Run a sharp knife along the edge of the ruler to cut the surface of the card but do not cut right through it. Fold the card away from the scored line.

Some suitable occasions for sending cards are listed below, but children will enjoy inventing others, as cards are such fun to make and send as well as to receive:

Cards can be made for birthdays of particular members of the family, such as a sister, father, uncle, grandparent, and so on; also for special birthdays, such as 1, 2, 3, 4, etc., 18, and 21; *bon voyage, congratulations*—on coming of age, engagement, wedding, anniversary, birth of baby, passing exams; *change of address, get well soon, good luck*—for exams, trips, driving tests, and so on; *special occasions*—Christmas, Chanukah, Easter, Father's Day, Mother's Day, Halloween, Valentine's Day; *invitations*—to parties, outings, dinners, and so on; *thank you*—for the party, the present, or your help; *welcome home, wishing you well*—in the new house or in the new job.

SIMPLE STUCK-ON PATTERNS

Organization

There will often be occasions when all the children will be involved in card making, for example, when a child or teacher

FIGURE 7-1
Simple stuck-on patterns

FIGURE 7-2
Birthday card

is ill and at such holidays as Christmas or Easter. As the materials involved are readily available, it is practical for card making to be a class activity. A pile of magazines can be placed in the center of each table and shared by the children at that table. Provide each group with a wastebasket so that a minimum amount of cleaning up is necessary when the cards are finished.

Materials

White cartridge or fairly stiff colored paper; scissors; glue and brush; sheets of colored gummed paper; old magazines; out-of-date calendars; seed catalogs; pressed flowers; doilies; pinking shears if available; tissue paper; paste and brush.

Technique

Fold a sheet of cartridge or colored paper in half to make the card. Decorate the front of the card by sticking things on. Flowers or flower pictures cut from a seed catalog, photographs or illustrations from magazines, or old calendars make attractive designs. Alternatively, patterns and pictures can be made by cutting out shapes from colored paper and sticking them on the card. For example, signs of the zodiac cut out in this way and glued

on the card make attractive and unusual birthday cards. A white doily glued onto a colored card and trimmed to size makes a pretty birthday or wedding card. The edges of the card can be trimmed with pinking shears to add further interest, but as cutting paper makes the shears blunt it is best to keep an old pair for this purpose.

Another possibility is to paste on shapes torn from colored tissue paper, as described in Chapter 5. This technique is particularly effective for fluffy Easter chicks on an Easter card.

CARD WITH OPEN WINDOWS

Organization

For younger children it is sometimes easier to have the basic card shape already cut out for each child. Older children should be encouraged to measure, cut, and fold their own papers to suit their individual designs.

Materials

Cartridge paper; ruler; scissors; pencil; glue and brush; crayons; paints and fine brush; felt-tip pens.

Technique

When the children first make these cards it is a good idea if they choose a fairly simple cover design, such as a tree or house which can incorporate several window shapes that open to reveal a message beneath.

Fold a sheet of cartridge paper to make the basic card shape. Make a rough plan for the front of the card, leaving adequate space for the windows. Use a ruler and pencil to draw the window shapes on the card. Cut the windows along three sides, leaving one side uncut to act as a hinge for opening. Cut out another sheet of cartridge paper the same size as the front of the card and glue it by the corners to the inside of the front page of the card. Fold back the windows and write a word or message on the space revealed beneath. Close the windows and decorate the card, using paints, crayons, or felt-tip pens. Further messages can be written inside the card.

CARD WITH A CONCERTINA FOLD

Organization

Before the children begin making their cards, they should always make sure that their hands are absolutely clean. A beautifully designed card will be completely spoiled by dirty smudges and fingerprints.

Materials

Cartridge paper; scissors; glue and brush; paints and brush; crayons or felt-tip pens; colored gummed paper.

Technique

Fold the cartridge paper to make the basic card shape. Decorate the front of the card, using paints, crayons, or felt-tip pens.

Open the card and use gummed paper

FIGURE 7-3
Card with open windows

shapes to create a character, such as a clown, policeman, or Santa Claus, on the inside. Leave a space where one arm or leg should be. Cut out a narrow strip of cartridge paper approximately half an inch (one centimeter) wide and fold it to make a concertina shape. Apply glue to one end of the paper concertina and attach it firmly to the card in the space left for the character's arm or leg. Cut out a small piece of cartridge paper in an appropriate shape, such as a star or heart, and write the card's message on it. Attach this to the free end of the concertina. Carefully fold the paper concertina until it is flat, and close the card.

When the card is opened, the paper shape bearing the message will spring out.

SHAPED CARD

Organization

In the introductory talk and demonstration the teacher must explain that when the picture is drawn on the folded sheet of cartridge paper, the design must include part of the fold so that this can be used as the card's hinge. For this reason it must be stressed that the children do not cut completely around their design but leave a section uncut at the card's fold. The design must have a flat base if the card is to stand up.

Materials

Cartridge paper; pencil; scissors; glue and brush; materials for decoration—gummed paper, material scraps, feathers, cotton, pipe cleaners; glue and brush; felt-tip pens.

Technique

Fold the cartridge paper in half and use a pencil to draw the shape required for the card. This could be an egg or rabbit

FIGURE 7-4
Card with concertina fold

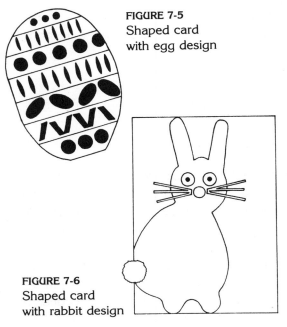

FIGURE 7-5
Shaped card
with egg design

FIGURE 7-6
Shaped card
with rabbit design

FIGURE 7-7
Shaped card
with bird design

for an Easter card; a butterfly, bird, or Christmas tree for other occasions. Remember to include a hinge for the card as explained above. Cut out the card along the pencil lines.

The egg can be brightly decorated with shapes cut from colored paper. The rabbit can be painted and whiskers added

by gluing thin strips of cartridge paper or pipe cleaners to his face. A cotton nose and tail will add to his charm. When the bird shape is cut out from the folded card, its wings are folded down on each side along the dotted lines to create the impression that it is flying. The bird's body can be decorated with paints, crayons, fur, or feathers. A small piece of paper bearing a message can be glued onto the end of the beak. If a length of thread is attached to the bird's neck, it can be suspended from the ceiling.

WINDOW-FRAME CARD

Organization

An accurately designed and well-made card looks both attractive and professional. Making window cards incorporates the mathematical skills of planning and measuring, and if this is done properly, the end result will be well worth the effort. The basic measurements and design for the card could be drawn on the blackboard for the children to copy.

Materials

Cartridge paper; scissors; glue and brush; paints and brush; ruler; pencil; crayons; felt-tip pens; magazines.

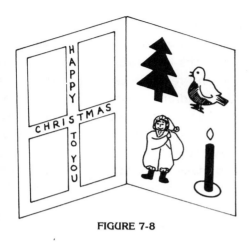

FIGURE 7-8

PADDED CARD

Organization

To avoid waste, each child in the group involved in this activity should be given a small piece of foam rubber for padding his own card. Although this will limit the design of the card to some extent, it will avoid the situation where one child cuts one large shape from the center of the foam rubber, leaving very little for the rest of the group. Foam rubber is an attractive material to children, so some of them might be greedy.

Materials

Cardboard; thin foam rubber; scissors; glue and brush; material; lace; tissue-paper scraps; dried seeds or beans; paints and brush; crayons; felt-tip pens.

Technique

Fold the cartridge paper to make the basic card shape. Using a ruler and pencil, carefully draw four window panes and cut these out of the front page of the card. Paint or crayon the window-frame shape on the front. In order to keep the inside of the card clean, open the card and place it face down on newspaper before painting the frame. A black or a brightly colored frame can be equally effective. When the decoration is dry, close the card and fill in each of the window panes with an appropriate design or glue on cutout pictures.

Open the card and write the message on the inside page along the horizontal and vertical spaces behind the window frame.

Cut the shape that is to be padded on the card from the thin foam rubber and glue it onto the card in the required position. Cut out the same shape in the material, but make it slightly larger than the foam-rubber shape. Carefully glue all around the edge of the underside of the material shape, place it on top of the foam rubber, and press the glued edge

FIGURE 7-9
Padded card

down onto the card so that the foam rubber is covered by material.

Decorate the outside edges of the padded shape by sticking on a strip of lace, dried seeds, dried beans, or tissue-paper scraps rolled into small balls, in order to cover all the glued edges of the material.

Decorate the remainder of the card, using paints, crayons, or felt-tip pens.

A border of lace or pretty ribbon all around the edge of the card will make it even more attractive.

REVOLVING CARD

Organization

When the children make more complicated cards they will need more help and guidance from the teacher. It is a good idea, when introducing a more sophisticated method, to give some alternative suggestions for cards which are easy to make and require simple materials. Not all the children will want to make elaborate cards, and this will enable the teacher to give more help where it is needed. For example, one group of children may like to make cards with distorted-looking messages, using perhaps very tall and thin or short and fat letters which are simple to make and amusing to decipher, whereas another group could be making revolving cards, which are more complicated.

Materials

Cardboard; paper; scissors; pencil; ruler; crayons; paints and brush; felt-tip pens; paper fastener.

Technique

Cut out two circles of cardboard and one circle of paper, all the same size. Fold the paper circle in half and then in half again. Use this quarter-circle shape to draw sections on one of the card circles, as shown in Figure 7-10, and draw a narrow border around the inside of the circumference.

Decorate each section with an appropriate design for the theme of the card,

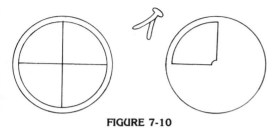

FIGURE 7-10

for example, Christmas or birthday scenes, seasons of the year, and so on.

Fold the point of the paper quarter circle over and use it to draw one section on the second card circle, as shown in Figure 7-10. Cut out this section. Place the second circle on top of the first circle and join them together with a paper fastener at the center. When the upper circle is turned, it will reveal different designs on the circle below.

A message can be printed on the upper card.

VALENTINE CARD

Organization

The teacher should demonstrate how to make this card before the children start on their own. It is also a good idea to show them a completed card, although the children need not copy the same design for themselves. It might well inspire them more than would a picture or verbal explanation. The teacher should suggest alternative means of decorating the cards so that some of the children will feel free to create their own designs. No special materials need be supplied for this if the children have access to the junk boxes and can use odds and ends from them for their decorations.

Materials

Thin cardboard; red tissue paper; tissue-paper scraps; doily; ribbon or velvet; scissors; glue and brush; felt-tip pens.

Technique

Cut a heart shape from a piece of cardboard and cover it with red tissue paper. This can be done by placing the card on the tissue paper and cutting around it, allowing a border of about three-quarters of an inch (two centimeters). Snip all around the tissue to meet the edge of the card, as shown in Figure 7-11. Fold each section of tissue paper over and glue it onto the back of the card. Cut out a circle from a doily and glue it onto the red heart, as shown in Figure 7-12. Cut out stems, leaves, and petals from tissue paper and glue these on or near the doily to resemble flowers. Two small, white heart shapes can be cut out and glued on each side at the top of the card. A valentine message can be written on them.

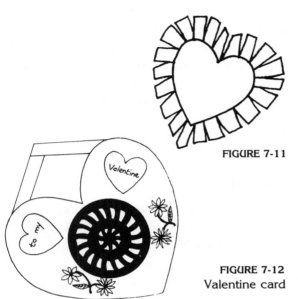

FIGURE 7-11

FIGURE 7-12
Valentine card

The card is hung from a short length of ribbon, velvet, or braid. Fold the ribbon in half and glue the ends onto the back of the card at the top, as shown in Figure 7-12.

EASTER CARD

Organization

For making cards and calendars in particular, it is a good idea for all the children in the class to pursue the same activity. This will enable them to share resources and discuss problems. The children should always consult and help each other when difficulties arise so that they are not solely dependent on the teacher. Often the best person to teach a child a new skill or explain how to solve a problem is another child.

Materials

Cardboard or cartridge paper; scissors; glue and brush; crayons; paints and brush; felt-tip pens; gummed paper; sponge; tissue; paste and brush; dried seeds; cotton scraps.

Technique

Cracked egg   Fold a sheet of cardboard or cartridge paper in half and cut out an egg shape, leaving a section of the fold intact. Cut a cracked egg line on the top page only, as shown in Figure 7-13, so that the card can be opened in two

FIGURE 7-13
Cracked-egg and hatching-chick cards

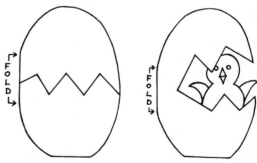

sections. Decorate inside and out with crayons, paints, felt-tip pens, or paper patterns. Write the message inside the card.

Hatching chick   Fold a sheet of cardboard or cartridge paper in half and cut out an egg shape, leaving a section of the fold intact as before. Cut a design to represent a cracked eggshell from the upper sheet of cardboard as illustrated. Cut out a small chicken shape from the spare cardboard. Glue the chicken behind the lower section of the crack so that it is clearly visible at the front of the card. Fold a small diamond shape of cardboard in half and glue it onto the chicken's face to resemble a beak. Decorate the card and chicken with paints, felt-tip pens, gummed paper or cotton scraps. Paint the chick's body yellow.

Standing-up chickens   To make a group of standing-up chickens, fold a piece of cardboard and cut from it the basic chicken design, as shown in Figure 7-14. Do this three times. Decorate the three pairs of chickens on one side only, using a sponge to dab on yellow paint or pasting yellow tissue paper onto the card. Paint the beaks and legs in a contrasting color and add eyes, using gummed paper, paints, felt-tip pens, or dried seeds.

Fold the chickens so that the decorat-

FIGURE 7-14

ed areas face each other. Join the three cutout pairs of chickens together by gluing them on their undecorated sides to form a group.

An Easter message can be written on the chickens' bodies or on pieces of paper glued at one corner and attached to their beaks. The chickens can be folded flat against each other to be put in an envelope.

CHRISTMAS CARD

Organization

Most children will enjoy making and giving cards that they have designed themselves. With commercially produced cards being so expensive, homemade

Christmas cards will enable each child to give original cards as well as enjoy making them.

Materials

Cardboard; pencil; scissors; glue and brush; aluminum foil; red acetate; gummed colored paper; paints and brush; crayon.

Technique

Robins Robins are made by using the same technique described for the standing-up Easter chickens, but as they are Christmas cards, the robins are covered with silver foil and given red breasts cut from red acetate or foil. The legs, beaks, and eyes are cut from gummed colored paper and stuck or glued onto the foil.

Christmas trees The Christmas tree card is a potato print with different tones of green paint used for the trees, which are superimposed on top of each other. The tree shape is cut from the flat surface of half a potato. Apply fairly thick paint with a brush to the cut potato and use it to print the tree design on the front of the card.

A handle can be cut from the upper curved part of the half potato, as shown in Figure 7-17, which will make printing with it much easier.

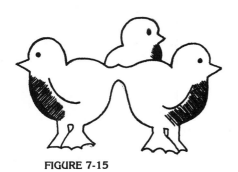

FIGURE 7-15
Robins

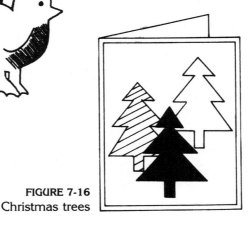

FIGURE 7-16
Christmas trees

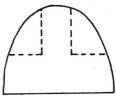

FIGURE 7-17

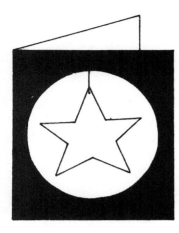

FIGURE 7-18
Hanging star

Hanging star   To make the card shown in Figure 7-18, fold a sheet of thin cardboard in half and cut a large circle from the center of one half. Draw a star shape on the spare circle of cardboard and cut it out. Paint or crayon the front page of the card or cover it with brightly colored gummed paper. Cover both sides of the star shape with silver foil. Make a small hole at one point of the star and another on the card just above the cutout circle. Tie thread through these holes to suspend the star in the circle.

Printing

Printing is a simple technique which can produce bold and effective results. It differs from other types of two-dimensional work in that the child will sometimes be making his or her picture with a knife or other type of cutting tool instead of a pencil or brush. Whichever approach used, the child is still drawing or painting his or her picture; it is only the instrument and the method that have changed.

One of the great advantages of a printed design is that it can usually be repeated as many times as required, using different colors and modifying the design between prints if desired. It can therefore be used when repeat patterns are needed for decorating wallpaper, curtains, notepaper, and so on. Also, many of the tools used for printing are extremely strong and will stand up to much experimentation and hard use.

Advanced methods of printing can be very sophisticated, but simple methods can produce equally good results. Printed patterns composed of just a few solid and simple basic shapes are often the most effective ones. The children will be fascinated by the many different ways of making a print and seeing how each printing technique produces definite characteristics of its own.

No special materials are required for

simple printing experiments. Many types of print can be made by using a thick mixture of the paint normally used in the classroom. This can be applied directly from a paintbrush onto the hand, piece of junk, vegetable, or string. For more advanced work, special printing inks can be bought from art and craft suppliers, but these are not necessary for beginners.

There are two main types of printing ink: one is water-based and is soluble in water for easy cleaning; the other is oil-based and is soluble in turpentine or petroleum spirits. Homemade printing ink can be made by mixing equal parts of powder paint and wallpaper paste to make a stiff, tacky mixture.

A selection of papers of various colors, textures, and absorbencies will be needed on which to take the prints. When printing ink is used, a roller will be needed for rolling out the ink on a board. Rollers need not be bought; suggestions for making your own are given later in this chapter. The printing ink must be rolled out onto a smooth surface, such as a sheet of glass, the smooth side of a piece of board, or a Formica tabletop.

Other equipment required for the techniques described in this section is cheap and readily available, if not already present in the classroom or from school supplies.

Finally, remember that successful printing will require much experimentation and this will inevitably create a certain amount of mess. It is therefore a good idea to cover the work tables and the surrounding floor area with sheets of newspaper before the work begins so that the children do not feel inhibited by the necessity to keep their work area absolutely clean and tidy.

PRINTING WITH PARTS OF THE BODY

Organization

When printing involves using parts of the body, supply the children with a bowl of warm water, soap, sponge, and a towel with which to wash themselves afterwards. It is unwise to use sinks for washing feet as accidents can easily be caused by the children slipping; water is also likely to be spilled on the floor.

Materials

Ink; roller; a piece of board or a Formica-topped table; cartridge paper.

Technique

Put a small quantity of the printing ink onto a smooth board or directly onto a

Formica-topped table. Use the roller to spread the ink evenly over the surface, adding more ink if necessary. Press hands, fingers, feet, or elbows onto the inked surface and then press them down onto a clean sheet of paper.

A picture or pattern can be built up on the paper in this way, or when the ink is dry, the prints can be cut out and glued onto another sheet of paper to make the design.

The tree picture in Figure 8-1 is made from handprints cut out when dry and glued together to resemble a tree. The tree trunk is a print made by a bare foot.

FIGURE 8-1
Picture made from hand- and footprints

PRINTING WITH JUNK AND VEGETABLES

Organization

Ask the children to bring a vegetable to school to use for printing. A potato is a good standby, but other fruit and vegetables will do equally well. Mushrooms and apples cut in half make good shapes to use. Experiment with sections of oranges, lemons, cauliflowers, and tomatoes.

Materials

All sorts of odds and ends from the junk box, including cotton reels, buttons, stones, twigs, leaves, feathers; selection of fruit and vegetables; knife; printing ink; piece of board; roller; paper.

Technique

Use the roller to roll out some ink onto a piece of board. If using a vegetable, cut it into segments or in half and firmly press down the part to be used for printing onto the inked board. Lift it up carefully and press the inked surface onto a sheet of paper. Follow the same procedure with items from the junk boxes.

A handle of Plasticine can be pressed onto a piece of junk to make it easier to hold when using it for printing.

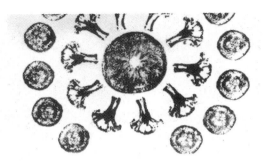

FIGURE 8-2
Printing with junk and vegetables

If leaves are used, choose those with well-defined veins on the underside, such as chestnut, ivy, and rose leaves. To make a more interesting potato print, cut the potato in half and use a knife to cut a design in the flat surface. To make the half potato easier to hold, cut away a section from each side of the curved surface as shown in Figure 7-17.

A potato print can be used to make a decorative border along one side of a piece of writing paper. A box of paper printed in this way would make an original present.

PRINTING WITH STRING

Organization

Allow a large uncluttered work surface for this activity and cover the surrounding area with newspaper. Ensure that each child has sufficient space in which to work and experiment without interfering with other children's work. Accidental splashes can easily spoil another child's picture.

Materials

For string printing, a thick mixture of powder paint and water is used instead of printing ink; plastic pot; string (not nylon); scissors; large sheet of white paper; thicker paper or thin cardboard for smaller prints.

Technique

Cut off a piece of string about 18 inches (half a meter) in length. Pour the paint mixture into an empty plastic pot. Holding an end of the string in each hand, dip the string into the mixture. Lift out carefully and allow the excess liquid to drip back into the pot. Hit, flop, twist, and loop the wet string on the surface of a clean sheet of paper. Superimpose one print on top of another, using a different piece of string dipped in a contrasting color.

Try putting a short length of string which has been dipped in the paint mixture in the middle of a folded sheet of thicker paper or thin cardboard with one end of the string protruding. Lightly hold down the folded paper with one hand

and carefully pull the string out by the protruding end. Open the folded sheet to reveal the design and allow it to dry.

Designs of this type made on a small sheet of cardboard can be used for illustrating calendars and greeting cards.

SYMMETRICAL PICTURES

Organization

A selection of different colored paints can be shared between several children. Keep one brush in each pot and use the brushes only for the pot of paint from which they come. If the same brush is used for more than one color, the paint colors will mix and will consequently be ruined.

Materials

Several colors of powder paint mixed to form a smooth, thick liquid; jars or pots; brushes; large sheets of cartridge paper; newspaper; roller.

Technique

Fold a large sheet of cartridge paper in half, open it out, and lay it on several sheets of newspaper. Use a paint brush to blob paint generously on the center

FIGURE 8-3
Symmetrical pictures

fold. Use several colors of paint in blobs positioned close to each other. Fold the sheet of paper in half again along the fold and press carefully all over the top page with the hands or a roller to spread out the paint. To some extent the design can be controlled by distributing the paint in specific directions, but haphazard designs can be equally effective and often more exciting. Carefully open the paper by peeling the pages apart and allow the symmetrical design to dry.

These patterns can be displayed without further decoration or used as the basis for further designs made with paint and inks applied with brushes.

Symmetrical pictures often suggest beautiful butterflies and flowers. They can be cut out when dry, and strings can be attached to each side to make exciting masks for the children to wear. Facial features such as hair, eyebrows, and beards can be added if required.

PRINTING FROM GLASS

Organization

If the printing activity is well supervised, sheets of glass with smooth edges and rounded corners can be used in the classroom. The work surfaces should be well covered with newspaper beforehand, and the teacher or an adult should place the glass on top of newspaper. If several tables or desks are pushed together, make sure the glass is not placed above the join where the tables meet but rests firmly on the flat surface of one table.

The children should be told that the glass must not be moved or picked up for any reason.

Materials

Sheet of glass; printing ink or thick paint; roller; candle; rag; tissue or piece of paper; stick; cartridge paper; newspaper.

Technique

Three simple techniques for taking prints from glass are given here. They can be used separately, or a combination of techniques can be used for one picture. With all these techniques, several prints can be taken without adding more paint to the glass.

1 Paint a design on a sheet of glass using a brush thick with ink or paint. Cover the design with a sheet of clean paper and place a second sheet on top to keep the print clean. Press all over the page with a hand or a roller; then carefully lift up the two sheets of paper to reveal the print. Place it, face up, on a clean, flat surface to dry.

2 Draw a design on the glass, using a candle or a wax crayon. Use a fully dipped brush to cover the surface of the glass with thick paint. The candle or crayon design will resist the paint. Take a print as described above.

FIGURE 8-4
Printing from glass—a rag has been used to "wipe away" the design

3 Apply a layer of paint to the entire surface of the glass and wipe a design on it with a rag, tissue, piece of paper, or stick. Take prints as described before.

Papers printed with any of the above methods can be used to cover a variety of containers to make attractive jewelery boxes, unusual pencil holders, and so on. The container should be varnished to protect the printed paper.

ROLLER PRINTING

Organization

If conventional rollers are not available, cylindrical cans with smooth sides and flat rims at both ends can be used as a substitute. Hold them at the ends, or alternatively, thread a piece of thick wire through a hole made in each end and bend it to make a handle, as in Figure 8-5. Strong cardboard tubes cut into sections of suitable length may also be used.

Materials

Roller; printing ink; piece of board; string; felt; scissors; glue and brush; cartridge paper; construction paper.

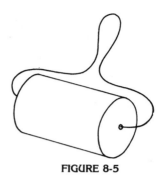

FIGURE 8-5

Technique

Three methods of using rollers for printing are described as follows:

1 The simplest way to print with a roller is to make the design with the roller alone. Put a small quantity of printing ink on a board or Formica-topped table and spread the ink evenly over the surface with the roller. Have the roller thick with ink to roll bands of ink in straight, curved, long, and short lines onto a clean sheet of construction paper. Continue in this way, using different colored inks, superimposing one color on another. Roller-shaped pictures often suggest mountains, fields, ships, and skyscrapers. Further details can be added later, if required, with ink or paint.

2 The second technique of roller printing is to cut out simple shapes in felt and stick them firmly onto the roller. The shapes could have a common theme, such as Christmas, animals, or people. When the glue has dried, dip the roller in ink and use it for printing in the usual way.

3 The third method involves the use of string. Spread glue all over the curved surface of the roller. Wind a length of string around the roller to make an interesting pattern, overlapping the string in places. When the glue has thoroughly dried, dip the roller in ink and use it for printing. Roll in several directions with long and short lines, some straight and some curved, using different colors to make an interesting print.

MONOPRINTING

Organization

Pieces of wood and board have many uses in art and craft work, and they are particularly useful for printing. Scraps can be bought cheaply from do-it-yourself shops and wood suppliers. The children may bring in pieces of wood left over from jobs done by their parents at home. The sizes of the pieces of wood need not be regular; varied shapes and sizes of wood will have different uses.

Materials

Printing ink; piece of board on which to roll out the ink; roller; sponge; matchstick or sharpened brush handle; paper.

Technique

Use the roller to spread the ink on the piece of board. Draw directly on the inked surface with a matchstick or the sharpened handle of an old paintbrush to make the design. Dampen a sheet of paper with a wet sponge and place it carefully over the inked drawing. Press evenly all over the back of the paper with your hand or use a roller. Remove the paper to reveal the print.

Many prints can be taken from the board without adding more ink. Experiment with different types of paper, for example, tissue and crepe paper. Try using a variety of tools to make the design, such as sticks, an eraser, and wooden pottery tools.

BLOCK PRINTING

Organization

The children might enjoy working together on one large picture using block-printing techniques. One method of printing can be used to make a picture or several methods can be combined.

Materials

Thick cardboard; scissors; glue and brush; printing ink; roller; cartridge paper; wood blocks; fairly thick string; felt.

Technique

The three methods described are block printing with a cardboard block, a wood-and-string block, and a wood-and-felt block.

Cardboard block   Cut out shapes from thick cardboard and glue them onto a piece of cardboard about the size of a sheet of writing paper. Let the glue dry. When ready, apply printing ink with a roller to the raised surface of the cardboard and lay a clean sheet of cartridge paper on top. Apply gentle pressure by rolling a clean roller over the covered surface of the cardboard block. Alternatively, press the cardboard block down onto the paper where the print is to be made.

Wood-and-string block   Cover one surface of a block of wood with glue and lay on it a piece of string in a pattern of lines and curves which do not overlap at any

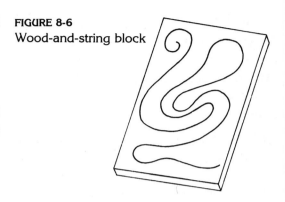

FIGURE 8-6
Wood-and-string block

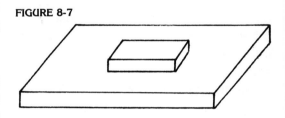

FIGURE 8-7

point. Use one piece of string or several pieces. When the glue is dry, press the block down onto an inked surface; then lift it up and use the inked block for printing on cartridge paper. Overprinting in different colors is particularly effective with a string block. For easier handling, glue a small piece of wood onto the back of the wood block and use it as a handle.

Wood-and-felt block   Cut out shapes from felt and glue them onto a block of wood as shown in Figure 8-8. Press the block face down onto an inked surface.

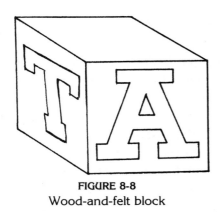

FIGURE 8-8
Wood-and-felt block

Lift it up and use it for printing on a sheet of cartridge paper. Letters cut from felt can be used to build up words. More than one surface of the wood block can be used for printing.

PRINTING WITH A PLASTER BLOCK OR POLYSTYRENE

Organization

At all times encourage the children to bring in useful junk items from home. As creative activities are developed in the classroom, the children will learn which items are of most use. Polystyrene trays of the sort used to package meat in supermarkets have many uses and are easily stored in the craft area.

Materials

Plaster of Paris; polystyrene trays with flat, untextured bases; one nail; used ballpoint pen; printing ink; piece of board; cartridge paper; roller.

Technique

Plaster block Mix up a small quantity of plaster of Paris as described in Chapter 3. Pour plaster of Paris into a polystyrene tray and leave it to set. When set, remove the plaster and turn the smoother side uppermost. Scratch a design in it with a nail or ballpoint pen. Roll out the printing ink onto the surface of a board and press the plaster block face downward on the ink. Lift it up and press the block down onto the cartridge paper to make the print.

Polystyrene Cut out the flat base of a polystyrene tray and use a nail or ballpoint pen to draw a design on the smoother side of it. Press the nail or pen into the polystyrene so that the design is clearly made, but do not pierce completely through the polystyrene. Use a roller to apply printing ink directly onto the patterned surface of the polystyrene. Press the inked surface down onto the cartridge paper to print the design. Alternatively, make the print by laying the

FIGURE 8-9
Printing with polystyrene

cartridge paper on top of the inked poly-styrene and applying pressure all over it with a clean roller.

CARDBOARD-SILHOUETTE AND STENCIL PRINTING

Organization

If it is not possible to obtain thick card-board for stencil printing, use cardboard cut from the side of a cardboard box.

Materials

Cardboard; scissors; cartridge paper; thick paint and brush; sponge; paper.

Technique

Cardboard-silhouette printing Cut a well-defined shape from a piece of thick cardboard. Animals, birds, people, and abstract shapes make suitable subjects. Place the shape on a sheet of clean cartridge paper and use a sponge dipped in paint to dab blobs of color on the paper all around the edge of the shape (see Figure 8-10). Carefully lift up the cardboard, place it in another position on the paper, and repeat the technique.

Stencil printing Make a stencil by cut-ting out a well defined shape from a piece of cardboard. Alternatively, cut sev-eral shapes from the cardboard to make a stencil design as shown in Figure 8-11.

Place the stencil on a sheet of paper and dab a sponge dipped in paint all over the cut-away area. Lift the stencil and make prints in other positions on the page, taking great care not to smudge the paint when the stencil is moved.

Other methods can be used to fill in the cut-away areas of the stencil. Try making prints with potatoes and items from the junk boxes, as described earlier, to fill in the spaces. Paint can be flicked from a brush onto the cutout areas of the stencil, or blobs of paint can be dropped and spread out by blowing

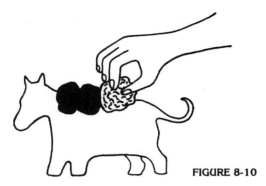

FIGURE 8-10

down a straw. An interesting effect is created by dipping a toothbrush in paint and pressing the bristles down on the paper all over the cut-away section of the stencil. Alternatively, place the stencil on construction paper or other colored or textured papers and use white or colored chalks to make the print.

CARBON-PAPER PRINTING

FIGURE 8-11

FIGURE 8-12
A stencil design

Organization

Whenever possible, encourage the children to experiment with their own ideas. When paper is involved in printing, it can be fun to try out the various techniques on different types of paper. This need not be expensive; a pile of paper, including wrapping paper, plain and patterned paper bags, and wallpaper, can be stored in the junk-box area for this purpose.

Materials

Construction paper and other types of paper; carbon paper; items from junk and material boxes; newspaper; roller.

Technique

Place a sheet of construction paper on the work surface and lay a piece of

FIGURE 8-13
Carbon-paper printing

after making prints in this way, traces of oil in the sink should be removed with a good cleaning agent.

Materials

Oil paints; turpentine; paper cups or empty yogurt cartons; tin tray or sink; paint brush; blotting paper; newspaper.

FIGURE 8-14
Marbled paper

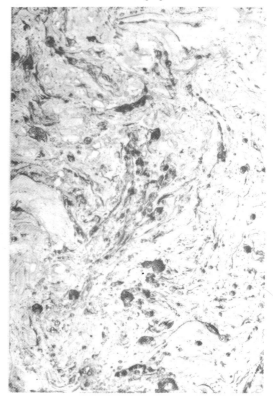

carbon paper face downward on it. Arrange a variety of objects on top of the carbon paper. These could include leaves, string, and textured fabric. Cover the objects with a sheet of newspaper and roll firmly all over the newspaper with a roller. Lift up the newspaper, objects, and carbon paper to see the print that has been made.

MARBLED PAPER

Organization

Rubber gloves are often useful for handling wet prints and for other messy jobs in the classroom. Aprons should always be worn and the children should also be reminded to roll up their sleeves before beginning their work. When cleaning up

Technique

Mix several colors of oil paint with turpentine and put each color in a separate container, such as a paper cup or empty yogurt carton. The consistency of the mixtures should be that of a syrupy liquid.

Half fill a tin tray or sink with water and pour small quantities of the paint and turpentine mixture onto the surface. Swirl the colors around with a paintbrush. Lay a sheet of blotting paper very gently on the surface of the water and after a few seconds lift up the paper, which should have a marbled design on it. Place this abstract, marbled picture on a sheet of newspaper and allow it to dry.

A stiff mixture of powder paint and cooking oil can be a substitute for the oil paints if these are unavailable.

Fabric Design

The basic technique used for making the tie-and-dye designs described in this section is quite simple. When fabric is folded, tied, and then dyed in one or more colors, the dye penetrates some areas and not others, giving highly individual effects and patterns. When the children first start to tie-and-dye material, the element of surprise is a great part of the fun. Later, as they get more experienced, they will enjoy controlling the results more closely.

No elaborate equipment is needed if a simple cold-water dye is used. An essential piece of equipment is a container large enough for submerging the tied articles in the dye solution. This could be a bowl, bucket, sink, or basin. Cold-water dyes and dye fixative can be bought from a variety of shops, including pharmacies and hardware and fabric retailers. If dye fixative is not available, baking soda can be used instead. Kitchen salt is also needed in the dye solution. A pair of rubber gloves will prevent hands from becoming stained with dye, and a large spoon or stick will be needed for stirring. A container will be needed for the first mix of dye and water. If a small box of dye is used, the container will need to be large enough to hold about half a quart (about half a liter) of water. As the container can easily become stained by the dye, it is a good idea to use a disposable one, such as a plastic soft drink bottle with its top cut off; but care must be taken not to knock the container over while it is in use as it is obviously not as stable as a jug or bowl.

When mixing the dye and dyeing material, always follow the manufacturer's instructions very carefully. These instructions should be included with the dye powder or liquid.

The results of these tie-and-dye experiments can be made into all sorts of attractive and useful articles, including scarves, curtains, handkerchiefs, headbands, aprons, and kites. For further experiments, basic tie-and-dye techniques can be combined on one garment or piece of material. For example, a scarf can be clump-tied at the center and knotted at the corners. More than one color can be incorporated into a design by binding the material again after each dyeing process has been completed and dyeing the material in another color.

Remember that results of tie-and-dye experiments cannot always be predicted very accurately, but accidents may be more exciting and effective than the planned design. All results can be used, whether to make an attractive garment, mat, or picture, or to provide patterned material scraps for collage or patchwork designs.

TIE-AND-DYE TECHNIQUES— KNOTTING

Organization

Tie-and-dye activities are suitable for groups of children working together so that the dye solution can be shared. The children should wear protective aprons and rubber gloves when using the dye. Remember, too, that traces of dye may remain on equipment used for mixing.

Materials

Cold-water dye; equipment for mixing the dye solution—a plastic soft-drink bottle with the neck cut off makes a useful container for the first mix of dye and water; an old dishpan can be used for a dye bath and the handle of a long paintbrush for stirring the solution; a cotton sheet cut into pieces of varying sizes makes suitable fabric for early experiments.

Technique

Make up the dye solution following the manufacturer's instructions. Tie knots at points on the material or at the four corners, as shown in Figure 9-1. Alternatively, roll the cloth into a long sausage and tie knots in this. For a more planned design, use a pencil or chalk to mark the position of the knots on the cloth before tying.

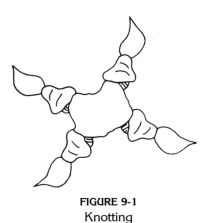

FIGURE 9-1
Knotting

Immerse the material in the dye for the length of time recommended in the instructions. Remove the fabric from the dye and rinse it well in hot, then cold, water until the rinsing water is clear. Untie the knots, allow the fabric to dry, and iron it flat. The parts of the material that were knotted should remain mostly undyed.

MARBLING AND PLEATING

Organization

Samples of fabric with different tie-and-dye techniques can be included in the same bath for dyeing. This makes the results twice as exciting.

Materials

Dye solution; cotton or linen material; thread; string; cord; raffia or rubber bands for binding.

Technique

Marbling Crumple up the fabric and bind it firmly with string to make a hard ball; leave several inches of string at the beginning of the binding. When the binding is complete return to the starting point and tie the two ends of string together. Dye the ball and rinse it thoroughly. Then, if more than one color is

FIGURE 9-2
Marbling

required, untie the ball and crumple up the material again. Bind it firmly and dye it in a second color. Allow the material to dry, unfasten the string, and iron flat.

Pleating   Gather the material in regular folds like a concertina and bind it at intervals along its length. It is easiest to use slip knots for the binding, carrying the thread from one knot to the next, as shown in Figure 9-3. Dye the fabric, following the manufacturer's instructions, and when dry, iron the material flat.

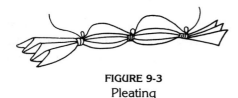

FIGURE 9-3
Pleating

TWISTING AND CLUMP TYING

Organization

Younger children may find it easier to work in pairs with this technique. Tighter knots and therefore more satisfactory results can be achieved when one child holds the material and the other concentrates on tying the knots.

Materials

Cold dye; material; rubber bands or string for binding; selection of objects for clump tying, e.g., stones, pebbles, marbles, beans, corks, coins, rice, and dried peas.

Technique

Twisting   Twist the fabric tightly until it coils back on itself like a skein of wool and bind it at the ends and at intervals along its length. Dye the material, rinse it well, and allow it to dry. Untie the knots and iron the material flat.

Clump tying   Wrap a stone or bean in the material and bind firmly below it with string or a rubber band as shown in Figure 9-5. Tie a variety of objects in the material in this way to make circular

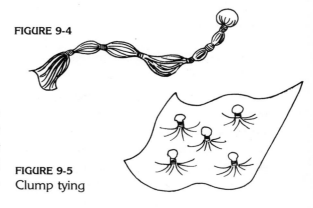

FIGURE 9-4

FIGURE 9-5
Clump tying

patterns when the material has been dyed. Dye the material, rinse it well, and allow it to dry. Iron it flat. Always follow the dye manufacturer's instructions carefully.

SEWING

Organization

It may be convenient to organize the class so that at any one time groups of children are working at different stages of the technique. One group could be preparing the fabric for dyeing, a second group could be dyeing their material, and a third could be making their samples into garments or mats.

Materials

Cold dye; material; pencil or chalk; needle; thread; scissors.

Technique

For a diamond pattern, fold the fabric in half and draw half-diamond shapes in pencil or chalk, as shown in Figure 9-6. Sew running stitches along the lines you have drawn; then pull the thread very tight in order to gather up the cloth. Dye the fabric carefully, rinse it well, and allow

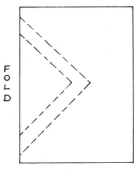

FIGURE 9-6

it to dry. Remove the thread from the material and iron it flat.

For a variety of effects, stitch different shapes on the material, such as hexagons, circles, and squares. The material can be stitched while it is flat or when it is folded.

BATIK

Organization

This activity is only suitable for small groups of children because the heating of the wax to boiling point and its use on the material must be carefully supervised by the teacher at all times. Always keep the work surface uncluttered to avoid accidentally knocking over the melted wax.

Materials

Two empty cans, one tall and one short, with the same diameter; small (birthday-cake) candle; large (power-failure) candle; soft paintbrush; fairly thin cotton material; newspaper; absorbent paper (large paper bags or wrapping paper will do); an iron.

Technique

Cut holes in the sides of the smaller can and remove its lid. Place the small candle inside it and balance the larger tin on top. Put an unlit candle inside the larger can and light the small candle.

Place the material on top of several layers of newspaper. When the candle has melted, dip a soft paintbrush into the wax and use it to make a design on the material. After every stroke of the brush, dip it into the wax and be sure that the wax has penetrated through to the other side of the material by holding the material up to the light. The waxed area should be transparent. When the wax is cold and set, immerse the material in a bowl of dye.

To make a crazy pattern on the cloth, crumple the material before immersing it in the dye to crack the wax. The dye will then penetrate where the wax is cracked.

Carefully dye the material, rinse it well, and allow it to dry. The waxed areas of the cloth will resist the dye. The wax can be removed by placing the material between layers of plain paper and carefully ironing over the whole area so that the paper absorbs the hot, melted wax. Replace the paper with clean sheets if necessary, until all the wax has been removed from the cloth.

Batik patterns are most effectively displayed in windows, where the light can shine through the wax-resisted areas.

Pottery

Clay is one of the most exciting and rewarding materials for children to use. It can be molded into abstract forms or made into objects for practical use. Some technical knowledge and skills must be learned, but with enthusiasm these are soon mastered. The techniques are learned gradually by working through each stage from raw clay to glazed and fired pot, tile, dish, or model. As the children gain experience in handling and treating clay, they will be more able to plan and control what the end product will be. However, early trial and error experiments are just as much fun and may produce exciting results. When the kiln is opened after the second firing and the glazed pottery is seen for the first time in its final form, the thrill experienced by both child and adult is enormous—even though the end product may bear little resemblance to the original design.

ORGANIZATION

It is advisable to reserve part of the classroom area for pottery activities and equipment. The clay must be stored in airtight buckets or bins with lids near to sturdy tables where the activity can take place. Much work with clay can be done on absorbent surfaces, such as paper towels or pieces of construction paper which will absorb some of the water in the clay and make it easier to handle. Shelves, cupboards, or a trolley are useful for storing equipment and finished work.

EQUIPMENT

Clay

A wide range of colored clays is available, but for beginners a choice of a red earthenware clay and a white clay is sufficient.

Tools

A collection of tools should include:

1 *Rolling pins.* These can be made by cutting wooden broom handles into sections about one foot (30 centimeters) long.

2 *Clay cutters.* To make a cutter for slicing the clay, wind each end of a piece of wire about 16 inches (40 centimeters) long around a toggle or small piece of wood. When small shapes need to be cut from the clay, a simple cutter can be made by pushing a hatpin through a cork.

3 *Straight wooden sticks* in pairs of equal thickness about 18 inches (half a meter) long. These are used for rolling out slabs of clay and can be bought as scraps from sawmills or lumber yards.

4 *Bowls* for water.

5 *A tool box* containing a wide selection of odds and ends for textured patterns and experimentation. It should include a sponge, a knife, spoons, stones, twigs, buttons, matchsticks, a comb, driftwood, textured paper, nuts and bolts, a spool, small blocks of wood, some paintbrushes, and string.

6 *Plastic or wooden modeling tools* and *heavy turntables* can be purchased later on for more advanced work.

BASIC TECHNIQUES AND MATERIALS

The basic technique for working with clay is as follows:

1 The clay is modeled and left to dry. This may take several hours or several days depending on the temperature of the room. At this stage it is called *greenware.*

2 When thoroughly dry it is put into the kiln for the first firing (biscuit firing), usually to a temperature of about 1760-1796° F (960-980° C), then left to cool in the kiln. It is now called *biscuitware*.

3 A selected glaze can now be applied to the biscuitware if desired.

4 The glazed biscuitware is put into the kiln for the *glaze firing*, usually to a temperature of about 1922° F (1,050° C) or more. After cooling, the finished article is removed from the kiln.

In the introductory sessions, basic skills should be demonstrated to small groups of children so that each pupil can clearly see how they are practiced.

Wedging

Before using the clay it must be wedged to remove air bubbles, which would expand during firing and shatter the clay. Wedging also ensures that the clay is of an even consistency so that the shape of the pot or model can be controlled. Wedge the clay by squeezing, rolling, and throwing it onto the work surface. The clay is ready for use if no air bubbles can be seen when the clay is cut with the wire clay cutter.

Crosshatching

Pieces of clay are joined together by crosshatching so that they will not fall apart as the clay dries. The surfaces to be joined must be roughened with a pointed stick, sprinkled with water, and then pressed firmly together with a twisting action to ensure a good join. All signs of the join can be smoothed over with a modeling tool or a wet finger.

Between sessions the clay must be kept damp if work is to be continued on it at a later stage. It can be placed inside a damp plastic bag, which is then sealed with a rubber band.

Clay that has dried out completely can be reconstituted, but it is hard work. It must be broken into small pieces and soaked in a bucket of water for several days. When the clay has broken down completely, pour off the surplus water and carefully dry the clay. To do this, place the wet clay on layers of newspaper or a slab of plaster of Paris until it is sufficiently dry to wedge and roll into balls.

Slip

Slip is a thick, creamy liquid of water and powdered clay which can be used for decoration and for joining two crosshatched surfaces together. It is made from dried, powdered, unfired clay that has been sprinkled onto water, stirred, and then sieved. Different-colored clays will naturally produce different-colored slips. Oxides, which can be purchased from pottery suppliers, can also be added to the slip to produce more colors.

Glazes

Glazes are supplied ready-mixed or in powder form. To make up the glaze from powder, sprinkle it onto water, using approximately one pound (450 grams) of glaze powder to three-quarters of a pint (0.4 liters) of water. When adding the powder, stir the mixture constantly to avoid the formation of lumps. The glaze should be the consistency of thin cream. If it is too thick, add more water. If it is too thin, allow the glaze mixture to settle and then pour off some of the water.

When the correct consistency has been achieved, pour the mixture through a hundred-mesh sieve (a sieve that has a hundred holes to each linear inch). Brush any lumpy residue through the sieve with a stiff brush.

Store the glaze in a closed container, such as a candy jar with a screw top or a bucket with a lid. Stir the glaze mixture every day and before use so that the glaze does not settle too long and harden.

Glazes can be transparent or opaque. Transparent glazes are used over slip or underglaze color decoration. The pottery can be decorated with underglaze colors which can be bought as sticks of color and used like crayons on the clay after the biscuit firing. Sometimes they are supplied in liquid form and applied with a brush to the damp clay before it is fired. A transparent glaze is then applied over the underglaze colors after the biscuit firing. Opaque glazes would obliterate any slip or underglaze design and are therefore used as a decoration in themselves.

It is possible to make colored glazes by mixing underglaze colors with transparent glazes, but this is a process of trial and error and success cannot be guaranteed.

When ordering clay and glaze supplies for children's use make sure that they contain no lead.

SOLID SHAPES

Organization

At first it is best to avoid a situation where only one group is allowed to use clay; otherwise the rest of the class will be distracted and frustrated in their desire to have a chance themselves.

Start pottery activities by demonstrating a simple technique to the whole class which can then be attempted by all the children at the same time, allowing ample opportunity for free play as well. In this way some of the initial excitement and eagerness of the children to try pottery for themselves will be satisfied. Newspaper should be placed on the tables and floor to minimize mess.

Materials

Red clay, as this is easier for beginners to handle; cutting tool, such as a knife or a piece of wire; pencil; some birthday-cake candles; flat stick.

Technique

Wedge the clay. Break off a piece of clay about the size of a child's clenched fist and work it well between the hands, rolling and pummeling it in order to get the feel of the clay. Begin to mold it into a solid shape, bearing in mind that the risk of accidents during firing will be increased if the shape is too large. The maximum thickness for safe firing of the clay is approximately one and one-quarter inches (three centimeters). To make the cylindrical paperweight (shown in Figure 10-1) roll the clay into a sausage and cut off a section with a knife.

Cubes and blocks can be made by either cutting the clay into shape with a knife or cutter or by hitting the clay on a flat surface to produce smooth, flat sides.

To make dice, press the point of a pencil into the sides of a cube of clay to make the dots, as shown in Figure 10-1.

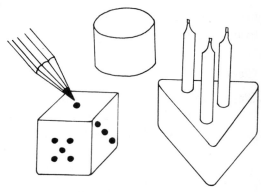

FIGURE 10-1
Paperweight, die, and candle holder

Small candles should be pressed into the clay while it is still damp to make the candle holder (Figure 10-1). After pressing the candles into the clay, move them around a little to create a slightly larger hole. This allows for shrinkage of the clay during firing. The candle holder makes an interesting centerpiece for a table at a child's birthday party.

SIMPLE MODELS

Organization

This activity is suitable for beginners. Usually, very little guidance is required from the teacher as the children will probably be bursting with ideas for things they want to make with clay. The first attempts should be practice sessions only; it should be understood that their work will not be put through the lengthy processes of firing and glazing until the children have acquired more skill and reached a certain standard in their work. This encourages the development of skills and minimizes wastage of materials.

Materials

Clay; box of tools; water; slip; paintbrushes.

Technique

Wedge the clay and break off a piece of manageable size. Mold the clay into the desired shape. If the clay becomes dry and cracked, smooth over the surface with a wet finger, but avoid getting the clay too wet. At first the children should be allowed complete freedom to experiment in designing their models or making abstract shapes.

After some initial modeling sessions, the children will want to make models that can be fired and glazed. They must be encouraged to avoid having the clay more than approximately one and one-quarter inches (three centimeters) thick because of the danger of accidents during firing and they must also be taught to crosshatch where clay surfaces are to be joined. Ideally, the form should be molded from one piece of clay, but in practice it is easier to join pieces onto the main shape, ensuring that the joins are carefully executed and secure.

The children should experiment with a variety of objects from the tool box to create interesting textured patterns on their models. Some simple slip decorations may be added before the biscuit firing by applying the slip with a soft brush.

FIGURES 10-2 and -3
Simple models

Another simple exercise for beginners is making a house number. Flatten a piece of clay by hand or with a rolling pin and use a sharp tool, such as a knife or clay cutter, to cut out the numbers required. When fired, the clay numbers can be attached to a piece of wood with strong glue.

THUMB POTS

Organization

This technique involves the use of the hands and fingers for molding and some simple tools for crosshatching. It is a good idea to arrange the tables or desks in the classroom in groups and cover them with several layers of newspaper. Then the groups can share a selection of tools and a bowl of water. Make sure that the bowl containing water is very stable so that accidental spilling is avoided.

Materials

Red clay; bowl of water; pottery tools; blunt knife; teaspoon.

Technique

Wedge a lump of clay about the size of a tennis ball and roll it on the table until it is more or less spherical. Cup it in the left hand and press the right thumb into the center to make a hole. Then gently rotate the ball of clay in the left hand. Squeeze the clay between the right thumb on the inside and the right fingers on the outside so that the walls of the pot will start to form and become thinner and taller as you work. Return to the base of the pot and use thumb and fingers to squeeze the clay from there up to the top.

Any cracks that appear, especially at the rim of the pot, can be smoothed away by gently stroking the clay with a damp finger, but avoid making the clay too wet or the pot will collapse.

When the walls of the pot are about half an inch (one centimeter) thick, flatten the base of the pot by gently tapping it on the tabletop.

Thumb pots can be made into sugar bowls, mugs, and money boxes.

An attractive mug can be made by adding a handle which has been securely crosshatched to the thumb pot. The child's name can be written on the mug with slip that is a different color from the clay used for the mug. For example, a name in white slip could be applied to a red-clay thumb pot. The inside of the mug must be glazed to make it nonporous if it is to be used for drinking.

Owls and pigs can be made by joining

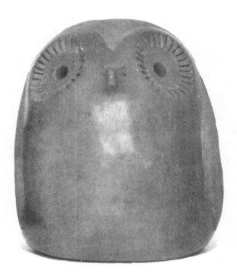

FIGURE 10-4
Owls made from thumb pots

two thumb pots together by carefully crosshatching around the rims of each pot. Press and twist the two rims together to ensure a good join. Remove any surplus clay at the join with a stick, knife, or pottery tool and smooth all over with a damp finger to hide all traces of the join.

To make an owl, flatten the lower thumb pot at the base, but keep the domed shape of the upper thumb pot for the owl's head. Make the owl's features with pottery tools and sticks and pencils. A blunt knife edge can be scraped on the surface of the clay to make a feather pattern.

Make the hollow thumb-pot shape into a pig by adding on shapes for legs, snout, tail, and ears. The ears can be joined to the head as flat triangles of clay and gently folded forward.

When two thumb pots are joined together in this way, an outlet must be created to allow air to escape during firing. This can be done by piercing eyes through the creature's head with a stick or pencil.

An attractive finish can be created on red clay by buffing the surface with the back of a teaspoon when the clay has partly dried out. The right degree of dryness may take several hours or even days, depending on the temperature in which the clay is stored. The best plan is to rub the clay at regular intervals until the buffing creates a slightly shiny surface. The more the clay is rubbed with a spoon, the better will be the results. This technique is particularly suitable for the owl's breast and around his eyes.

MOLDED DISHES

Organization

Each child will need a polystyrene tray, but other equipment, such as rolling pins and sticks, can be shared by a group working together on a large work surface.

Materials

Piece of cloth on which to roll out the clay (this can be a piece of burlap or thick cotton); two sticks of the same thickness; rolling pins; polystyrene trays (the type used for packaging meat in supermarkets); clay cutter or knife; sponge; water.

Technique

Take a lump of clay about the size of a clenched adult fist and wedge it. Place the clay on the cloth, which has been spread on the table, and lay the two sticks on either side of it about one foot (30 centimeters) apart, as shown in Figure 10-5. First, flatten the clay by hand; then use the rolling pin to roll the clay flat until the rolling pin rests on the sticks and the slab of clay is an even thickness. Carefully lift the slab of clay off the cloth and drape it over the polystyrene tray. Gently ease the clay into the shape of the tray, taking care to avoid finger marks on the surface of the clay. Use a wet sponge to ease the clay into the contours of the tray and to give the clay a smooth finish.

Use the knife or clay cutter to trim off the surplus clay around the edges of the tray. The edge of the clay can be cut at an angle to make an interesting rim. The dish provides an excellent surface for slip decoration while the clay is still damp and supported by the polystyrene tray. Also, attractive textured patterns can be made on the clay while it is still damp, using fingers or a variety of objects from the tool box. As it dries, the clay dish will shrink away from the polystyrene tray and it can then be taken out and put into the kiln for firing. The outer edges of the rim can be trimmed and neatened by gently running a metal rasp along them to remove any rough or jagged fragments of dried clay.

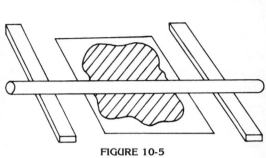

FIGURE 10-5

FIGURE 10-6
Molded dish with slip decoration

TEXTURED PATTERNS ON TILES

Organization

Before the children make their own designs, it is a good idea to take them on an outing to see how textures and patterns have been used creatively to decorate the environment. Look on public buildings, churches, and town halls for raised and incised designs.

Materials

Clay; piece of material for rolling out the clay; two sticks of even thickness; rolling pin; clay cutter or knife; assorted tools for incised patterns and crosshatching; bowl of water.

Technique

Roll out the clay on a cloth placed between two sticks as described in the section on making a molded dish. Cut out a clay tile, but keep it to a manageable size as the larger it is the more difficult it will be to handle. Gently press down with a finger all around the edges to reduce the risk of warping.

Use your fingers and hands to make designs on the clay by pressing and pinching, or make patterns on the clay surface with such objects as twigs, leaves, stones, string, a comb, buttons, a thimble, and pottery tools.

Raised patterns can create abstract or real designs as shown in Figure 10-7. These designs are made by attaching clay shapes to the tile, making sure to cross-hatch thoroughly where the two surfaces are to be joined.

If the finished tile is to be hung, make a hole near to the top by pressing a smooth-sided pointed stick completely through the clay slab. It is essential that the clay tile is dried very slowly so that it does not crack or warp. To do this, leave it to dry in a very cool place for several hours; then gradually move it to warmer places until it is thoroughly dry and ready for firing.

Abstract textured patterns on clay tiles may look best unglazed, and the natural clay colors are often most effectively displayed out of doors, for example, in a playground or garden.

A group of children could make tiles based on a theme such as "The Sea," with the tiles depicting scenes of mer-

FIGURE 10-7
Textured patterns on tiles

maids, ships, fishes, Neptune, and so on. When the tiles are colored and glazed attractively, they can be mounted in a block or panel, possible forming part of a background for a topical display.

RESIST PATTERNS

Organization

Before the children attempt their own designs using a resist technique, discuss

with them the possibilities of design and texture. Make a display of objects to stimulate their interest and provide ideas. This could include pebbles patterned with curved lines and sections of vegetables. A pencil or charcoal drawing can serve as a plan before the design is transferred to the clay.

Materials

Clay; piece of material on which to roll out the clay; two sticks of even thickness; rolling pin; clay cutter or knife; paper towels; scissors; bowl of water; sand or

FIGURE 10-8
Resist pattern made with rough sand

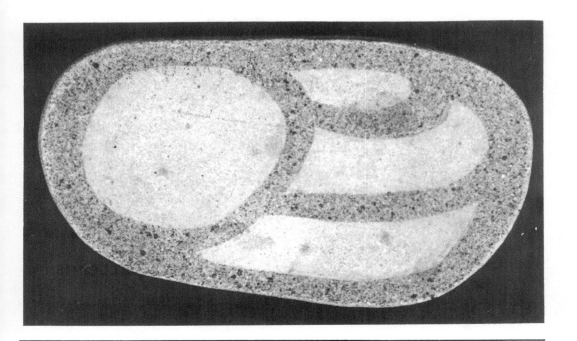

grog (fired clay that has been broken down into fairly coarse or fine powder); block of wood with a flat surface covered with a layer of fine cloth or burlap.

Technique

Roll out the clay on a cloth between two sticks as described previously. Cut the clay into a regular or irregular shape, such as a tile or pebble. Plan a design where some areas of the clay will remain undecorated and some areas will be patterned with the sand or grog. The areas to remain undecorated must be covered with damp paper towels cut to the shapes which are to resist the textured decoration.

Carefully lay the wet cutout paper shapes on the clay slab in the required design, and while the paper is still wet, sprinkle sand or grog all over the clay. Then use the covered woodblock to pat and press the sand or grog into the surface. Dry the clay slabs slowly to avoid the risks of cracking and warping. When thoroughly dry, shake off the surface sand or grog and remove the paper. After the biscuit firing, a transparent glaze may be applied if required.

This method of creating a design by using a resist technique can also be adapted by using slip instead of grog or sand. In this case, the paper must be pressed well into the clay to keep it in place when the coating of slip is poured over the dish.

Resist decorations can also be made by pressing flowers or leaves into the damp clay and applying the slip, grog, or sand in the usual manner.

JEWELRY

Organization

Making things to wear always appeals to children, especially when the object has a professional look and the child can explain how it was made. Pottery pendants, badges, belts, and bracelets will appeal to both sexes for they can make presents for others as well as things for themselves.

Materials

Clay; bowl of water; rolling pin; piece of cloth or paper towel; tool box containing odds and ends for making textured patterns; clay cutter or knife; leather thongs; long shoelaces; wool or braid; safety pins; insulating tape.

Technique

Roll out the clay on a piece of cloth or paper towel until it is a fairly thin, even thickness. Carefully cut out the shape required for a pendant or badge. For a belt, cut out several shapes of equal size to make the sections of the belt (see Figure 10-9). Neaten all edges by smoothing gently with a damp finger. Make holes where necessary by pushing a stick completely through the clay, or cut them out with a clay cutter or needle while the clay is still wet. Apply a decoration by using slip, or press string, buttons, or odds and ends from the tool box into the clay to make a textured or impressed design. Allow the clay to dry slowly to prevent warping and cracking. After the biscuit firing apply a transparent glaze. After the glaze firing, when the pottery has cooled, attach the thongs or shoelace to the pendant so that it can be worn. Thread the required length of thong or shoelace in and out of the belt sections and finish off with a knot. Bracelets can be made with the same technique.

For a brooch or badge, use a short length of insulating tape to attach a safety pin to the back.

FIGURE MODELING AND MORE ADVANCED MODELS

Organization

As the children develop new skills and confidence in handling clay they will naturally advance to more ambitious projects. They must always remember that good wedging is essential and that the bulk of the clay must not be too thick in order to ensure safe firing.

More advanced models may develop naturally from practice and experimentation. It is a good idea to reserve one space in the classroom near the activity area for a display of models, pictures, and postcards to serve as a stimulus.

FIGURE 10-9
Belt and pendant shapes

FIGURE 10-10
Examples of figure modeling and more-advanced models

Materials

Clay; water; modeling tools; slip; underglaze colors; soft paintbrush.

Technique

Wedge a bar of clay of the required size and mold the figure or model, taking great care that all joins are securely crosshatched. Models must be put in a cool place and allowed to dry out very slowly as the possibility of cracks appearing is a very real danger. Red clay is most effectively used for figure modeling and left without slip or color decoration so that the form of the model is emphasized. However, some areas can be decorated with white slip before the biscuit firing. White clay models can be decorated with underglaze colors. Where slip or a color decoration is involved, a transparent glaze can be applied after the biscuit firing to give a more finished appearance.

MODEL SCENES

Organization

A theme might develop from topic work or from pictures and photographs displayed in the classroom. It could be an activity related to the theme of "my home," or "my holiday" or an item in the news, such as "space exploration." The children will be able to utilize skills already learned, so it should be unnecessary for the teacher to provide much assistance or guidance. Often the best results are achieved by a child working quietly alone or with a partner in a corner well away from the distractions of other pupils or the help of a teacher. If the child is totally absorbed in the activity and the model is developing well, try to allow as much time as he or she requires to work on it. No craftsman enjoys having his or her work interrupted when totally involved in a task, and a strong creative drive cannot easily be revived after an enforced break.

Materials

Red or white clay; modeling tools; rolling pin; piece of cloth or paper towels; bowl of water; clay cutters; underglaze colors; transparent glaze.

Technique

The model consists of a scene supported on a slab of clay for a base. The clay base is rolled out with the rolling pin so that the clay is approximately even in thickness. Press down lightly with a finger all around the edges to prevent warping.

The figures are modeled and carefully attached to the base by crosshatching. Larger objects such as houses and space rockets can be shaped by using the thumb pot technique as previously described.

Hollow shapes joined to the base of the model must have an outlet for expanding air to escape during the firing. These can easily be made as windows, doors, or a chimney.

While the model is still damp, use a soft brush to apply the underglaze colors if they are supplied in liquid form. Do not apply liquid underglaze colors when the clay has thoroughly dried out before the biscuit firing because the introduction of moisture to the dry clay will cause it to crack. If the underglaze colors are supplied as sticks, use them very gently as the clay will be fragile. Alternatively, use the underglaze color sticks after the biscuit firing, before applying a transparent glaze and putting the pottery into the kiln for the glaze firing.

SLAB POTS

Organization

This technique should be demonstrated to small groups of children so that they can clearly see how the cylinder is made.

FIGURE 10-11

Again, the importance of crosshatching when joining the features to the cylinder face can be emphasized.

Materials

Clay; cardboard cylinder to use as a mold; clay cutter or knife; box of tools; cloth on which to roll out clay; rolling pin; sticks; small clay cutter.

Technique

Roll out the clay on a cloth between two sticks as previously described. Cut out a rectangle of clay that is the same width as the height of the cardboard cylinder that is to be used as the mold. The rectangle of clay must be long enough to wrap around the cylinder. Allow a little extra clay to overlap at the join. Carefully roll the clay around the cylinder, allowing about a half an inch to an inch (one or two centimeters) to overlap. Trim off the surplus clay at the join and at each end of the cylinder. Crosshatch where the ends of the clay meet at the join. Sprinkle a little water on the roughened surfaces and press them together firmly. Smooth over all signs of the join with a wet finger. This cylinder provides the basis for the model.

To make the man shown in Figure 10-12, use spare pieces of clay to make his

FIGURE 10-12
Slab-pot man

features and a thumb pot to make his hat. Crosshatch thoroughly where the features are attached to the cylinder to prevent them from falling off as the clay dries. The cardboard cylinder can be carefully removed before the biscuit firing

FIGURE 10-13
Candle cover

or left in place to burn away during the firing process. The clay can be left unglazed after the biscuit firing or it can have a slip or underglaze decoration with a transparent glaze on top.

To make the candle cover shown in Figure 10-13, cut away some shapes from the cylinder to make an interesting pattern. After the biscuit firing, place a candle on a tile or upturned can lid and place the cylinder over it. When lit, the candle light shines through the spaces. This can make an attractive centerpiece for a dinner table.

COIL POTS

Organization

This is another skill that should be demonstrated to small groups of children at a time so that each child can see clearly how the technique is performed. As the children develop skills in handling the clay they will be eager to learn new techniques, and coiling is a good introduction to more sophisticated work. If possible, make the coil pot on a heavy metal turntable; these can be bought from the clay suppliers. The children will enjoy using the turntable, and it will enable the pot to be turned easily as the sides are gradually built up. Do not restrict the children to small-scale work; a competent and practiced child will get great satisfaction from making a large jug or pot. However, this will require sustained effort on the part of the child and frequent checking for sound work on the part of the teacher.

Materials

Red or white clay; rolling pin; clay cutter or knife.

Technique

Roll out a small slab of clay for the base of the pot. A circle of clay about three inches (seven centimeters) across is a good size to start with. Aim for an approximately even thickness of clay for the base. Use the clay cutter to cut out the base of the pot and crosshatch all around its circumference on the upper surface. Use fingers to roll out a piece of clay into a long sausage or coil about half an inch (one centimeter) thick; lay it around the base on top of the crosshatching and press down firmly. Build up the side of the pot by laying one coil of clay on top of another, as shown in Figure 10-14, taking care not to create air holes between the coils. Roll out more sausages of clay when they are required. If a large supply is rolled out at the beginning, they may become dry and crack as the work on the pot progresses. A small supply can be made at a time and kept damp by sponging them with water or by covering them with a damp cloth or paper towel.

After laying every two or three coils, carefully smooth down the inside and outside of the pot with a finger until the coils are merged together and the surface is smooth.

Continue building in this way until the pot is the required height. To bring the

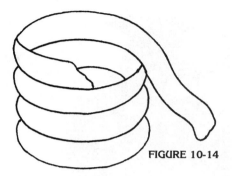

FIGURE 10-14

sides in, when modeling the neck, for example, gradually position the coils closer to the center of the pot.

To make the sides of the pot splay out (when making a bowl, for example), place each coil a little further out from the center than the previous coil.

A common fault in making a cylinder is that the walls of the pot spread out like a bowl because of lack of skill in controlling the form. Correct this by cupping the pot between the hands and gently easing the sides of the pot inward until they stand up straight.

Lips for jugs can be stroked out with a wet finger and handles can be made from a section of a clay coil joined to the pot at each end by crosshatching.

Textured patterns can be applied with a variety of tools, or the pot can be decorated with slip or underglaze colors while the clay is still damp before the biscuit firing.

FIGURE 10-15
Coil-pot jug

A transparent glaze applied after the biscuit firing will make the pot nonporous.

SLIP DECORATION

Organization

Using slip for decoration on clay can be very messy, especially at first when the children are experimenting. It is essential to reserve a large uncluttered work surface covered with several layers of newspaper or a plastic cloth for this activity.

Slip can be purchased ready-mixed from a pottery supplier, or if bought in powder form, it can be mixed by the children in the classroom. It is constantly needed for both making and decorating pottery so it is worth mixing up quite a large quantity at a time.

Materials

White slip; red slip; paintbrushes; jug; wooden board; dishpan; bowl of water; sponge; nail; screwdriver; knitting needle; modeling tools; slip trailer; feather.

Technique

Slip must always be used on damp clay; if it is applied to clay that has dried out it will cause cracking.

Slip decoration can be applied by simply "painting" the slip onto the clay with a soft-haired paintbrush. It will be necessary to keep dipping the brush into the slip so that the brush does not churn up the surface of the clay and discolor the slip. Try using brushes of different thicknesses for varied effects. Contrast thin lines with thick lines and smooth curves with sharp angles. Experiment as much as possible until the desired effect is achieved. The slip can be wiped off with a damp sponge to prepare the surface for further experiments.

FIGURE 10-16
Slip decoration on molded dishes

For some methods of slip decoration it is necessary to coat the whole surface to be decorated with a thin covering of slip. To coat the surface of a tile, for example, place the tile on a board or tray and hold it at a slight angle over a dishpan or bucket. Pour slip from a jug over the tile so that the excess slip is collected in the container below and can be returned to the slip bucket.

For the inside of a dish or thumb pot, the pot is half filled with slip, which is then tipped and rolled about until the slip just touches the edge all round the pot and the excess slip can be poured out. Any unwanted blobs of slip can be removed with a damp sponge. To coat the outside of the thumb pot with slip, hold the base of the pot with a finger and thumb and then dip it in a bowl of slip. When the slip coating is dry, a design can be scraped in the slip to reveal the color of the clay underneath, making a sgraffito decoration. Different tools can be used to scrape the slip away; for example, screwdrivers, knitting needles, nails, or modeling tools will produce different effects.

A slip trailer is a spherical plastic container with a nozzle at the end. To fill it with slip, remove the nozzle and squeeze the air out of the container. Place the open end in the slip, release the pressure so that it fills itself, and replace the nozzle.

The slip trailer can be used to trail a design of lines and blobs on a damp clay surface. The tip of a feather can be swept across parallel lines of slip to produce an interesting effect.

To make a marbled pattern as shown in Figure 10-17, pour a small amount of slip into a dish or bowl; then use a slip trailer or brush to drop blobs of slip of a contrasting color on top of the first quantity of slip. Hold the bowl in both hands and gently tip it from side to side so that the slip colors run into each other and make the marbled pattern. After the bis-

cuit firing, apply a transparent glaze to the inside of the bowl so that the design will show through clearly after the glaze firing.

GLAZING BY DIPPING AND POURING

Organization

Glaze is applied to pottery that has cooled down after the biscuit firing. The surfaces to be glazed must be clean and dry.

Glazing usually requires close supervision by a teacher or experienced older child. It is not always easy to remedy mistakes made during glazing so it is best to ensure that the job is expertly done at the time. It is essential to check that the base of a pot is wiped clean of all traces of glaze before the firing; otherwise the melted glaze will stick to the kiln shelf during the firing and both pot and shelf will be ruined. Glaze can be purchased ready-mixed from a pottery manufacturer or supplied in powder form and mixed according to the manufacturer's instructions. Always stir the glaze before use.

Materials

Glaze; bucket; bowl of water; sponge; two flat sticks.

FIGURE 10-17
Slip used to make a marbled pattern

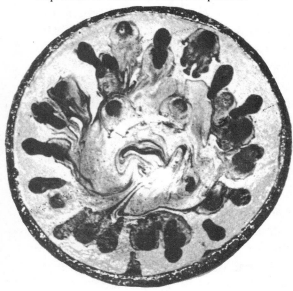

Technique

To glaze the inside of a pot, pour some glaze into the pot, swirl it around until it has reached all the area to be glazed, and pour off the excess. For the outside of the pot, hold the pot upside down by the base, using one finger and thumb, and dip the pot into the glaze. Hold the pot in the glaze for about three seconds and lift it smoothly out, allowing the drips to drop back into the bucket. Hold the pot in this position for a few minutes until the glaze dries; then carefully place it on its base on a clean, dry surface. Finger marks can be covered by dabbing them with a soft paintbrush dipped in glaze. Wipe the base clean of glaze with a damp sponge.

Shallow dishes can be glazed by this method or by sweeping them through the glaze in one steady motion. Larger pots and models can be glazed by placing them on sticks suspended across the top of a bucket, as shown in Figure 10-18. The glaze is poured from a jug over the pot, and the glazed pot is allowed to dry while still in this position. When dry, any small areas missed by the glaze can be touched up with a paintbrush and the base wiped clean of all glaze with a damp sponge. The excess glaze collected in the bucket is returned to the glaze container.

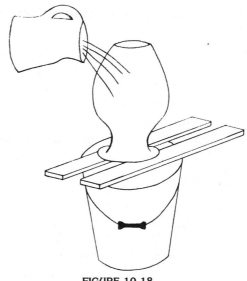

FIGURE 10-18

Tiles and flat surfaces such as pendants can simply be lowered face down into the glaze, held for a few seconds, and then lifted out and allowed to dry.

Should the whole operation of glazing go wrong and the glaze appear blotchy and uneven, wash the glaze off under the faucet and let the biscuit-fired clay dry out thoroughly before repeating the process. In this case, any underglaze color decorations beneath the glaze will have to be repeated.

When unsatisfactory results occur, the glazed pottery can be broken down into fragments for making mosaic patterns and pictures. The following are some common faults in glazing and their likely causes:

Fault

1. Milky appearance of glaze
2. Bubbling on glaze
3. Cracked glaze
4. Patchy areas: some glazed, some un-glazed

Cause

1. Glaze too thick or firing temperature too low
2. Firing temperature too high
3. Kiln allowed to cool too quickly
4. Glaze too thin or greasy areas on bis-cuitware

GLAZE EFFECTS WITH COLORED GLASS

Organization

This activity involves breaking up colored glass bottles and jars. If this is done by the children, close supervision will be necessary and the suggested precautions that follow should be taken so that the risk of accidents is minimized.

Materials

Colored glass bottles and jars or marbles; thick paper or cloth bag; hammer; plastic tub to use as a safe container for the broken glass; spoon; white clay; pottery tools.

Technique

Use fingers and pottery tools to make a solid block of clay and then hollow out a bowl shape in the middle, as shown in Figure 10-19. Place the bottles or jars to be broken inside a very thick paper bag. The paper must be strong and thick enough to contain the glass when it is hit with a hammer. Alternatively, use a bag made of strong cloth. Seal the opening of the bag with a rubber band or string and hit the bag with a hammer until the glass has been broken into small pieces.

FIGURE 10-19

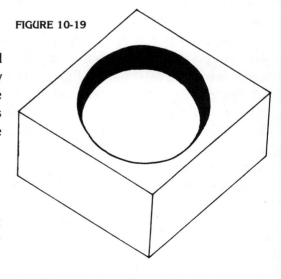

Tip the broken glass out of the bag and into a plastic bowl. Use a spoon to put some fragments of glass into the hollowed-out bowl in the clay. Put the clay form containing the glass fragments into the kiln for a glaze firing.

Marbles can be used instead of glass fragments, and these have the advantage that they need not be broken. During the firing the glass fragments melt and fuse together to make an attractive, colorful design. This glass may craze and crack during cooling, but this can produce even more interesting effects in the finished bowl.